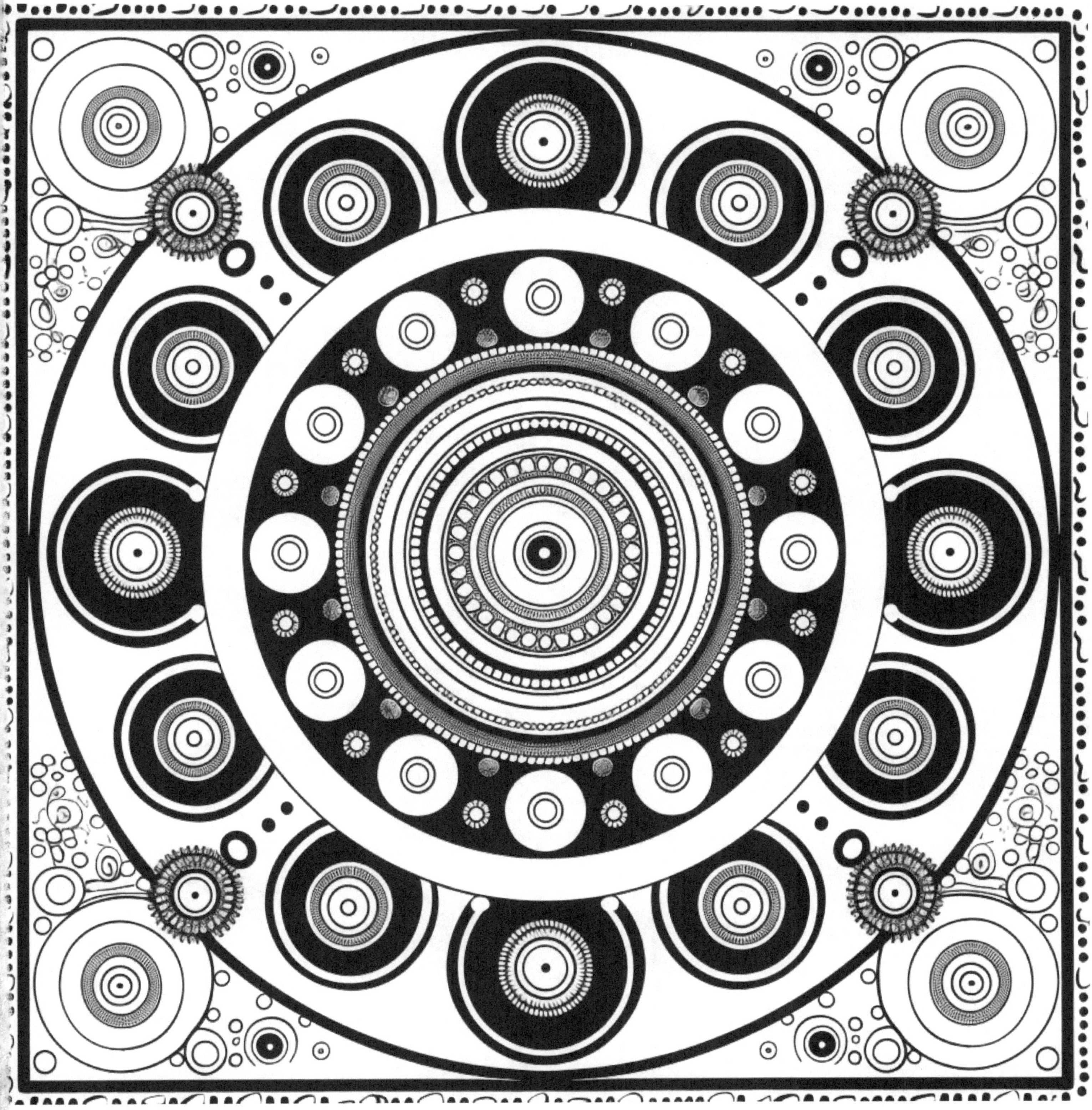

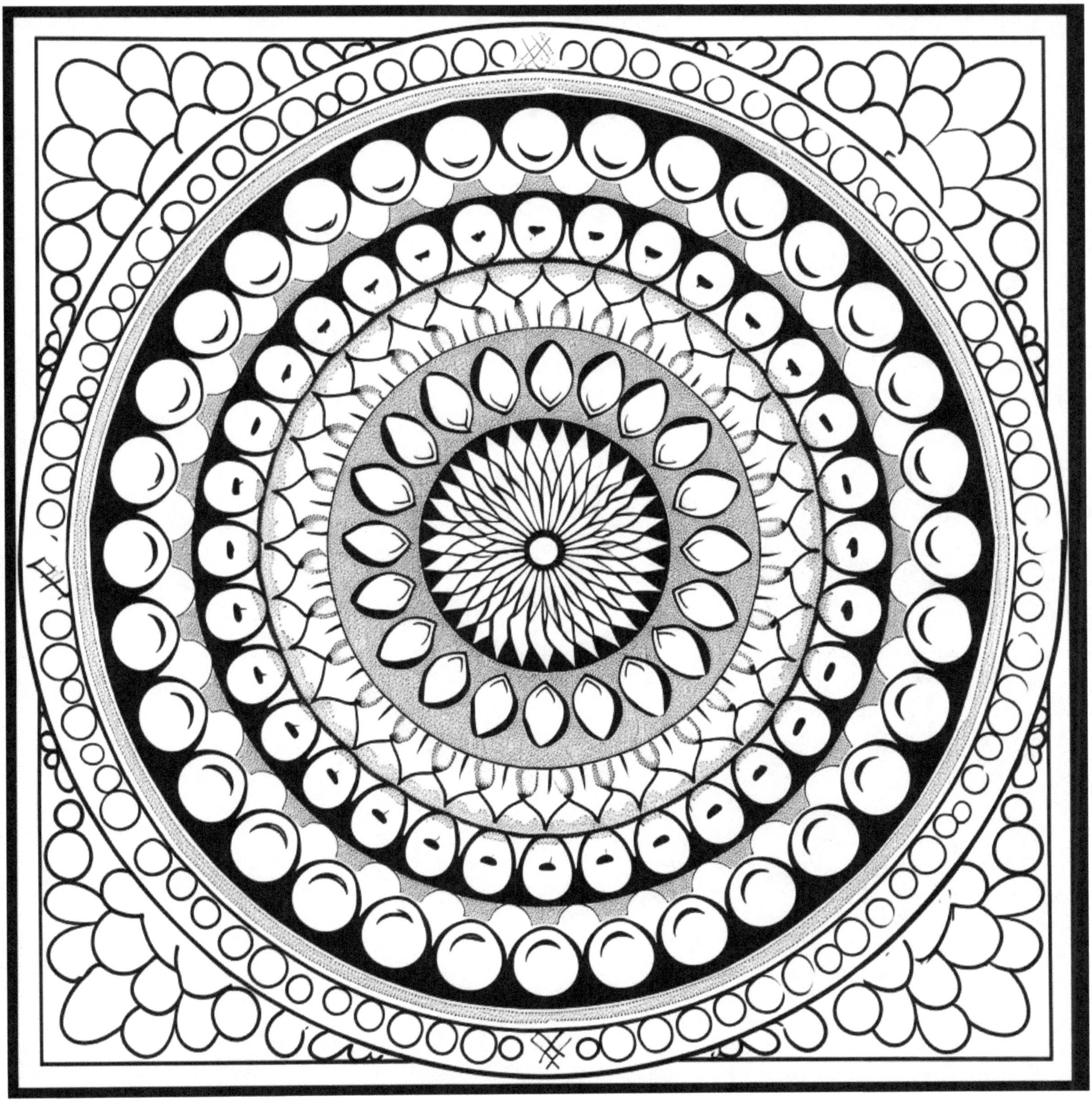

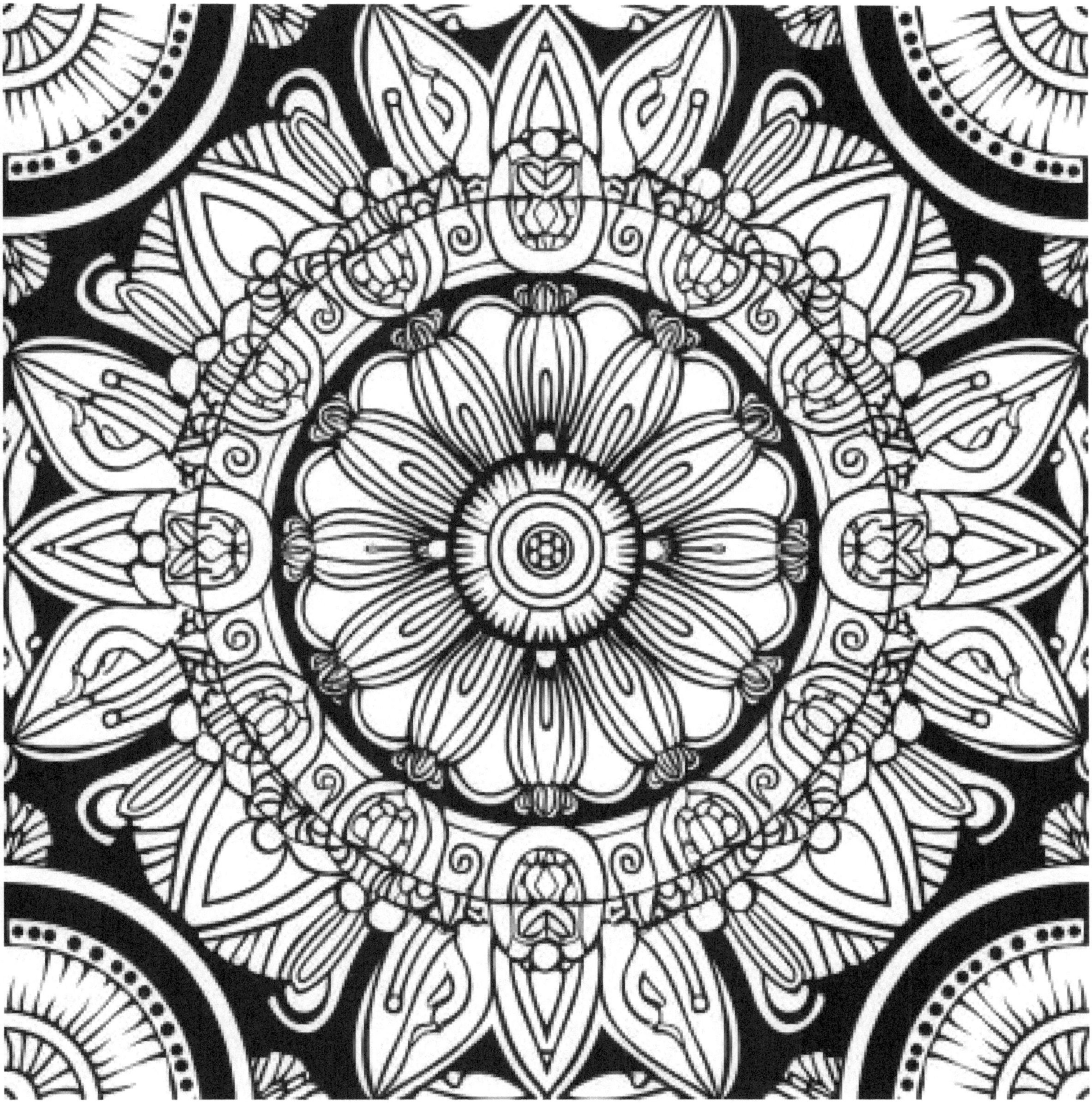

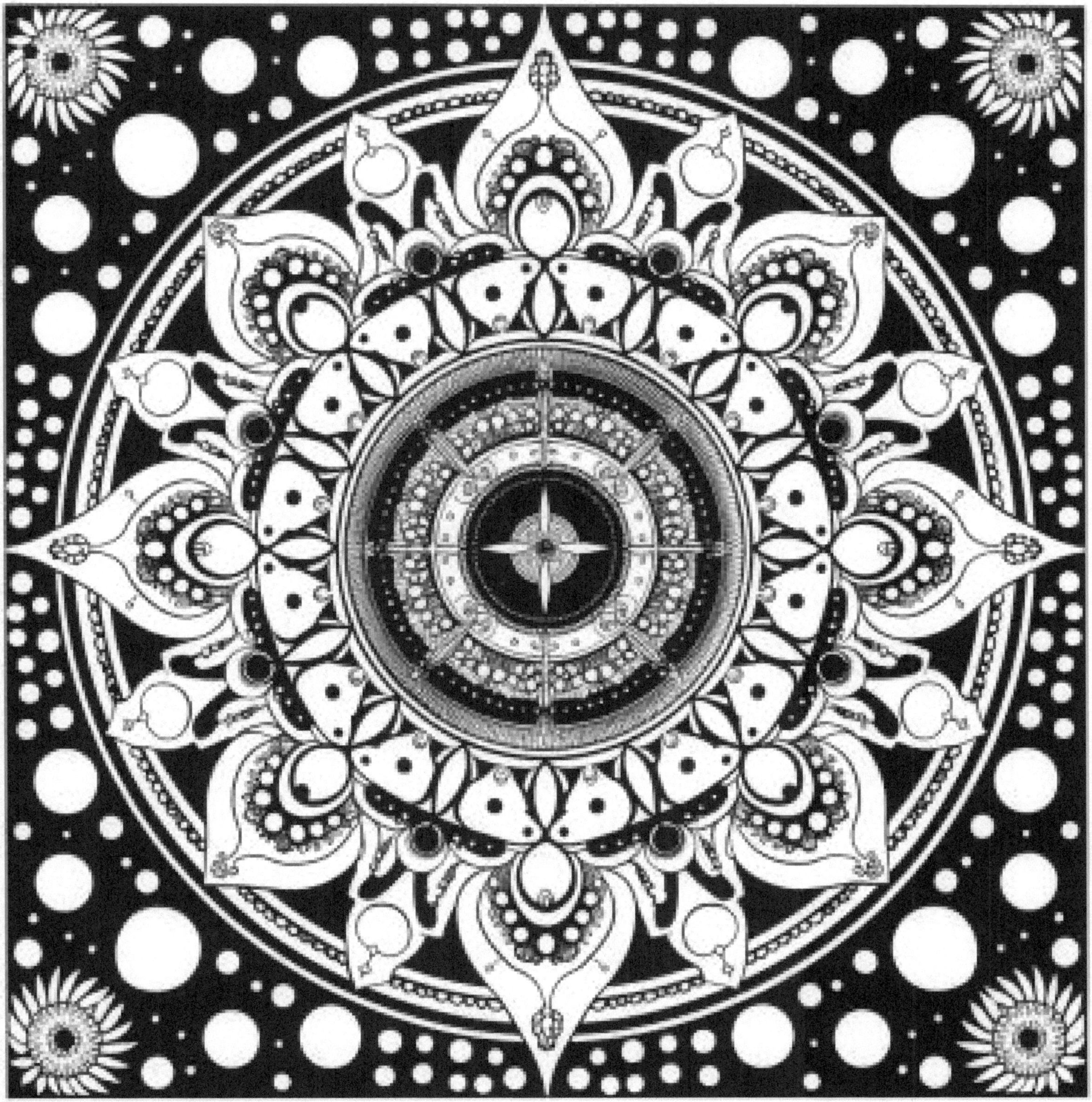

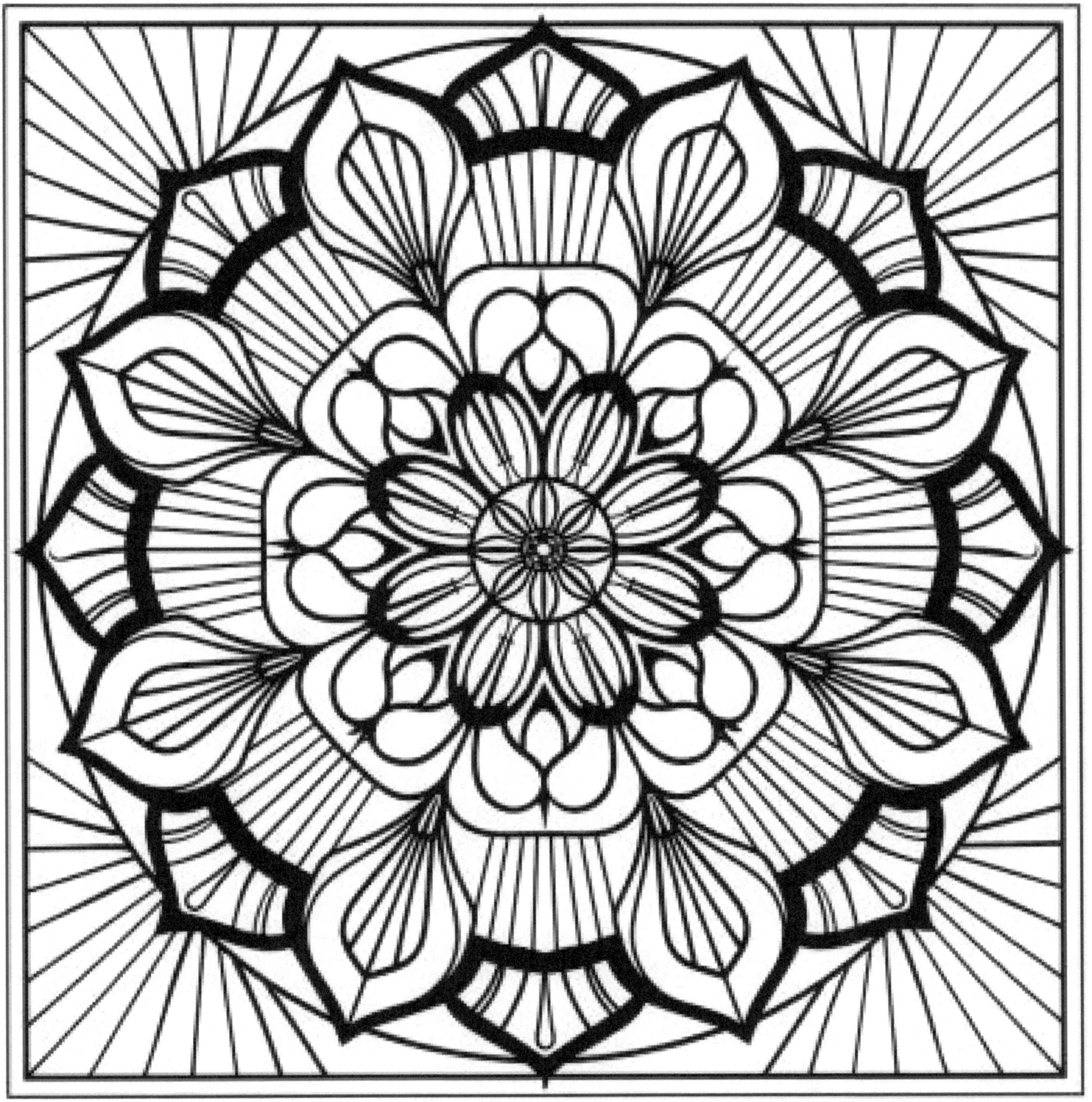

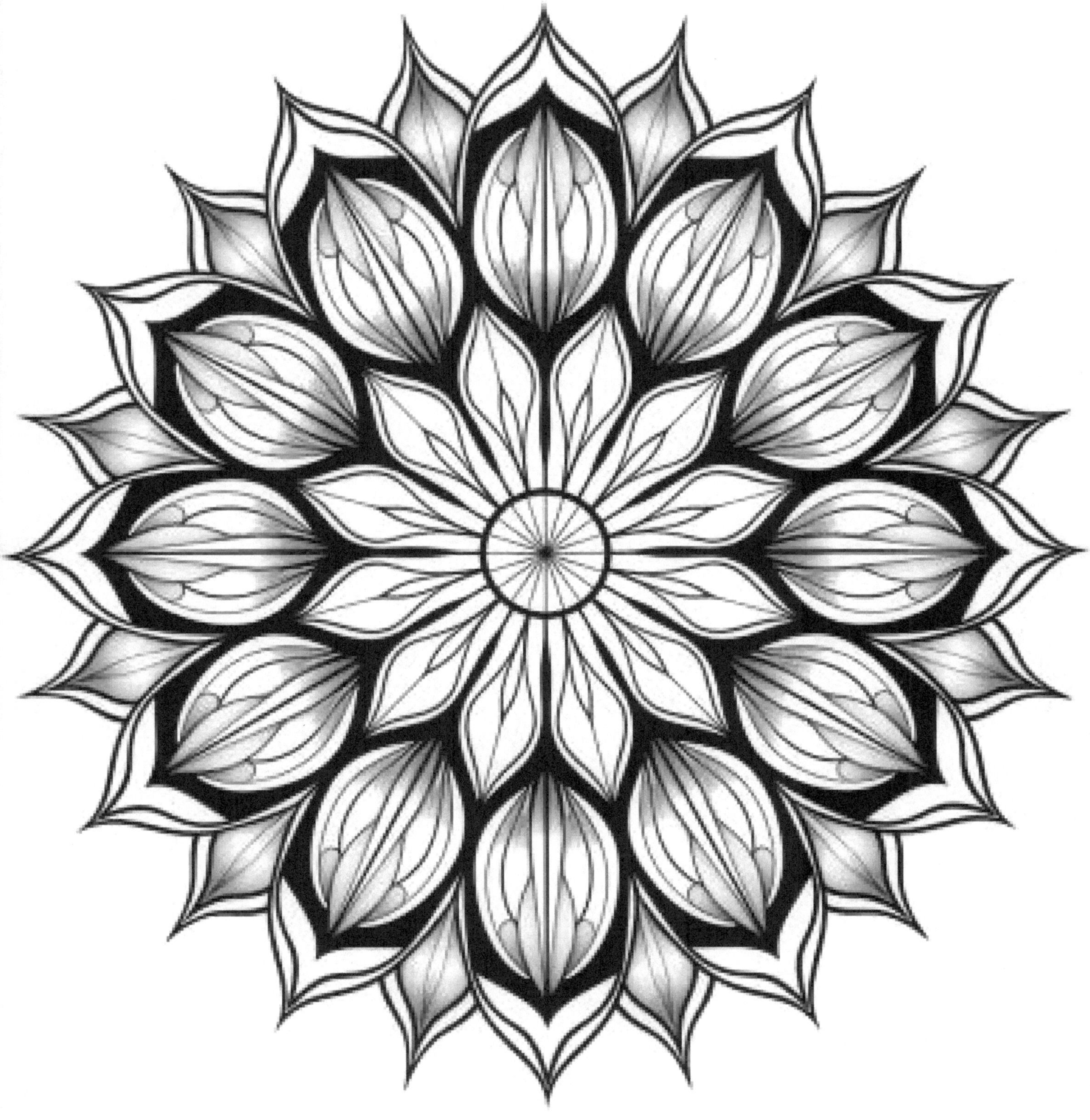

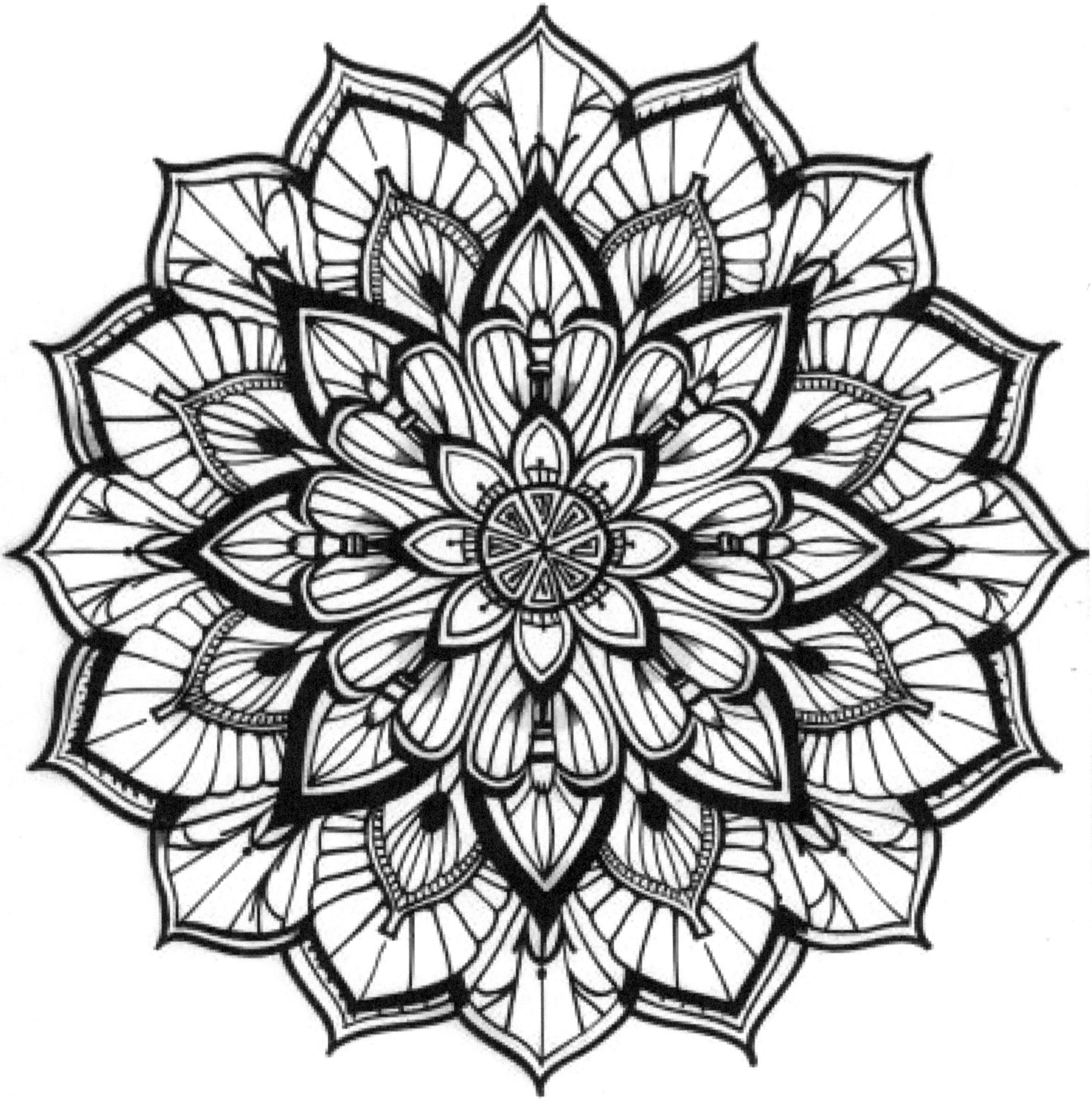

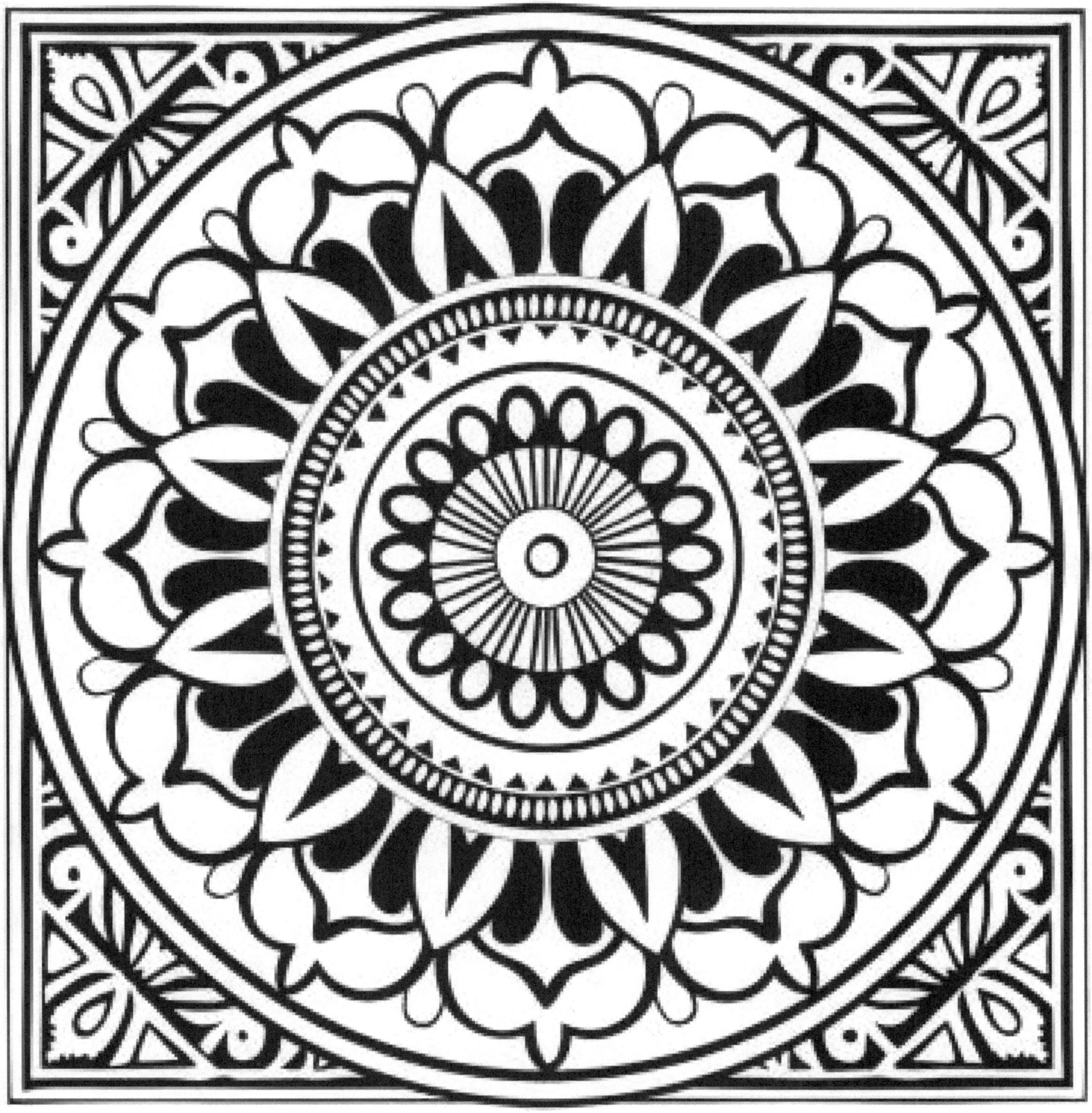

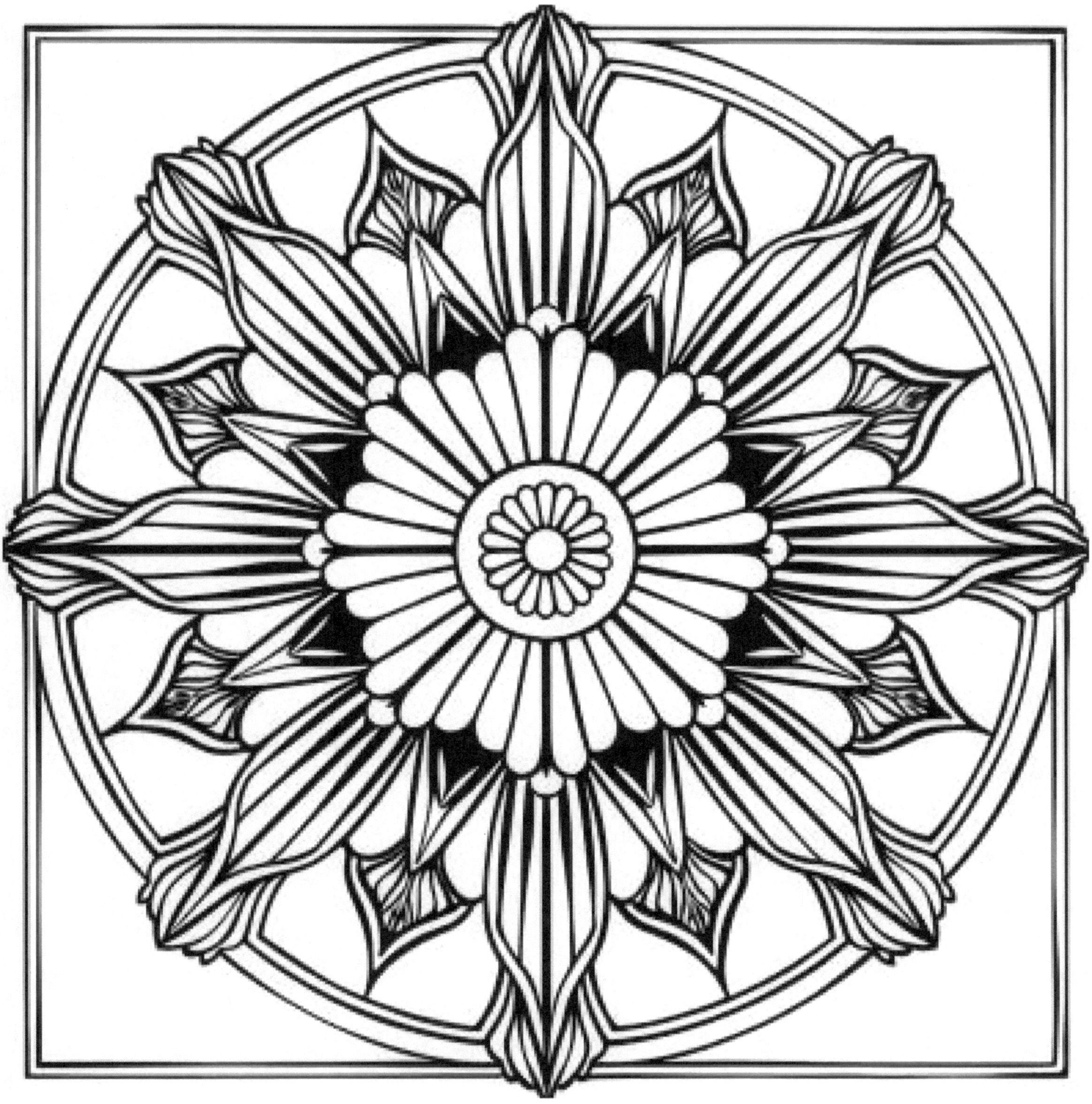

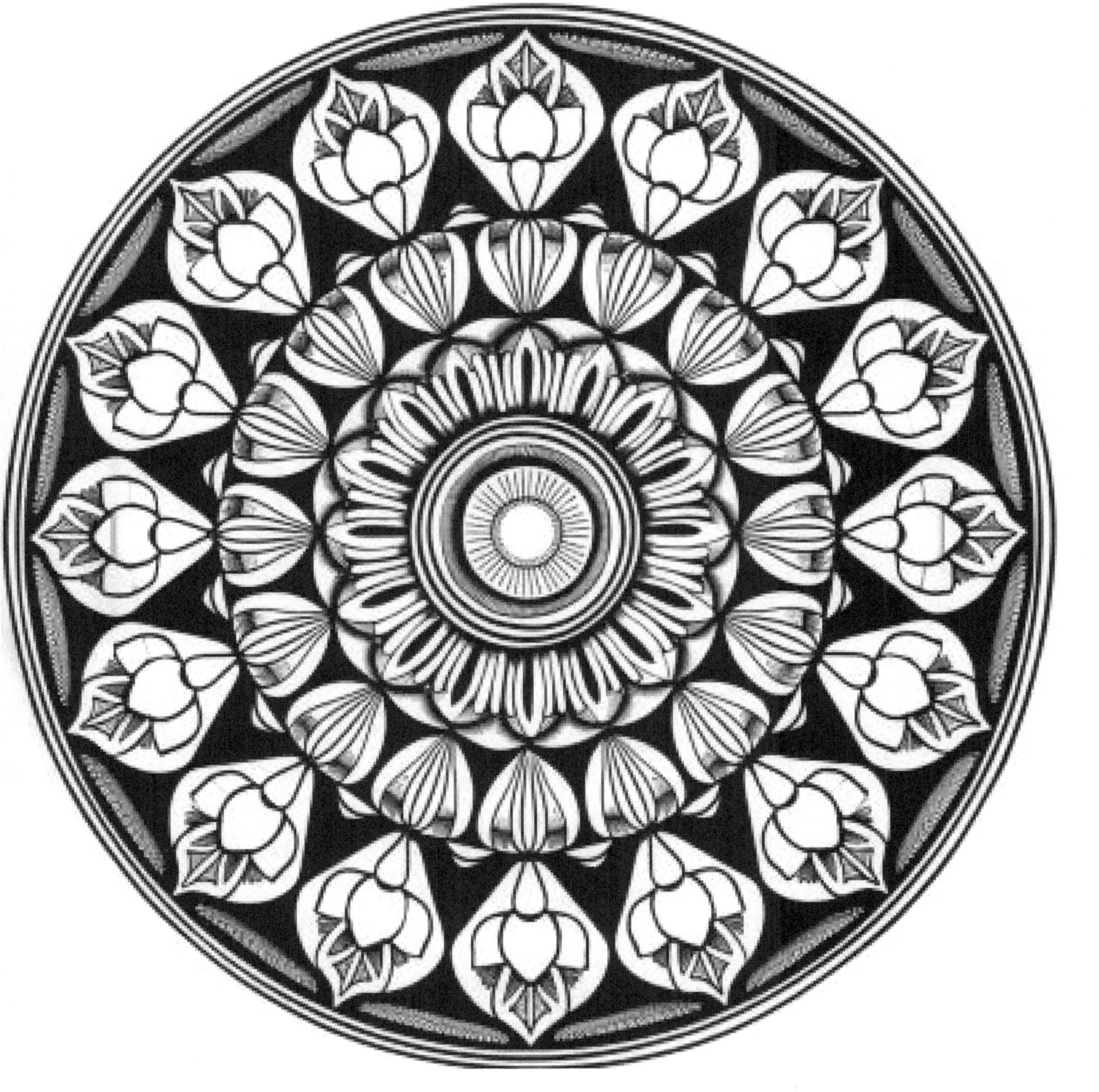

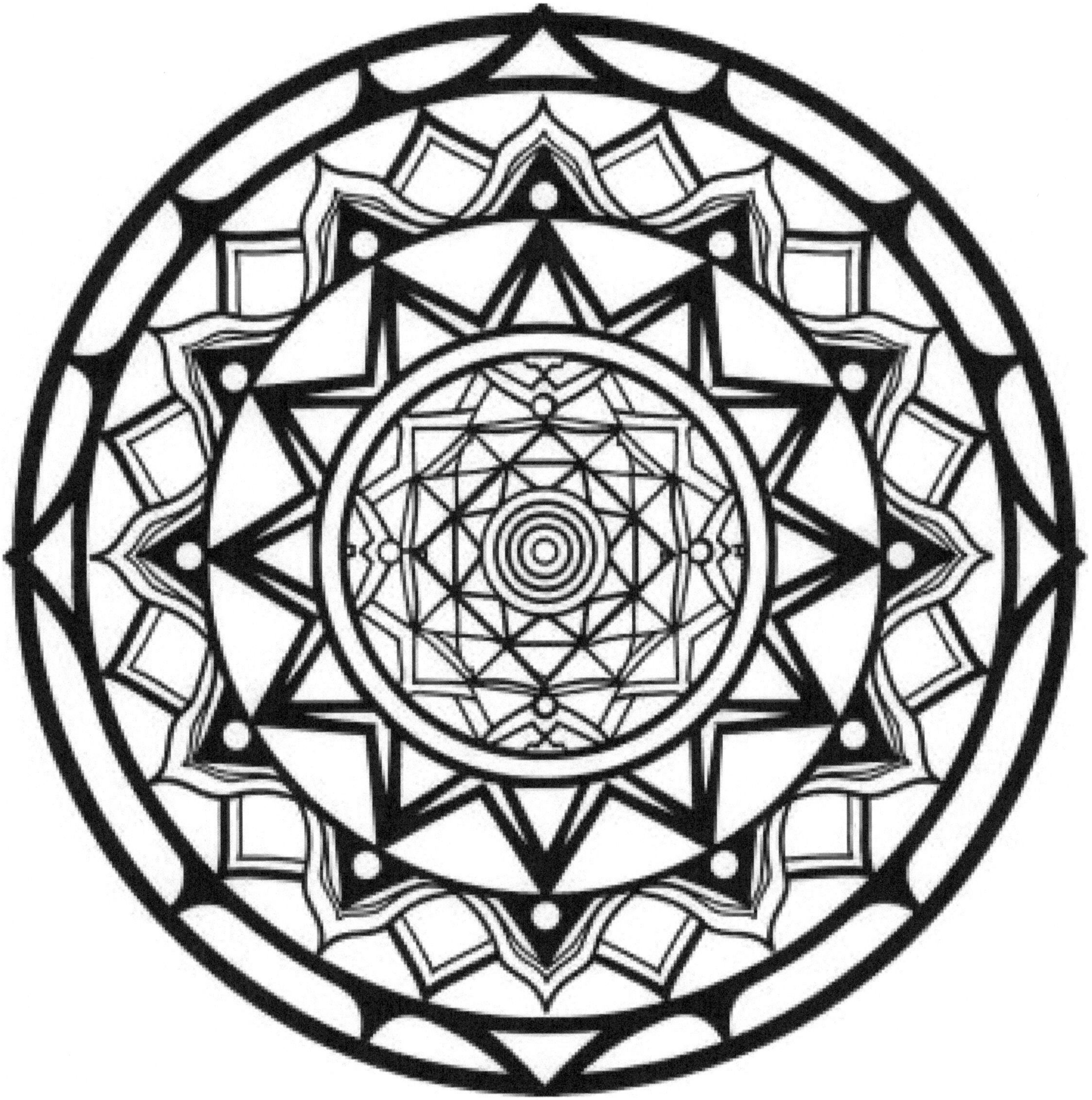

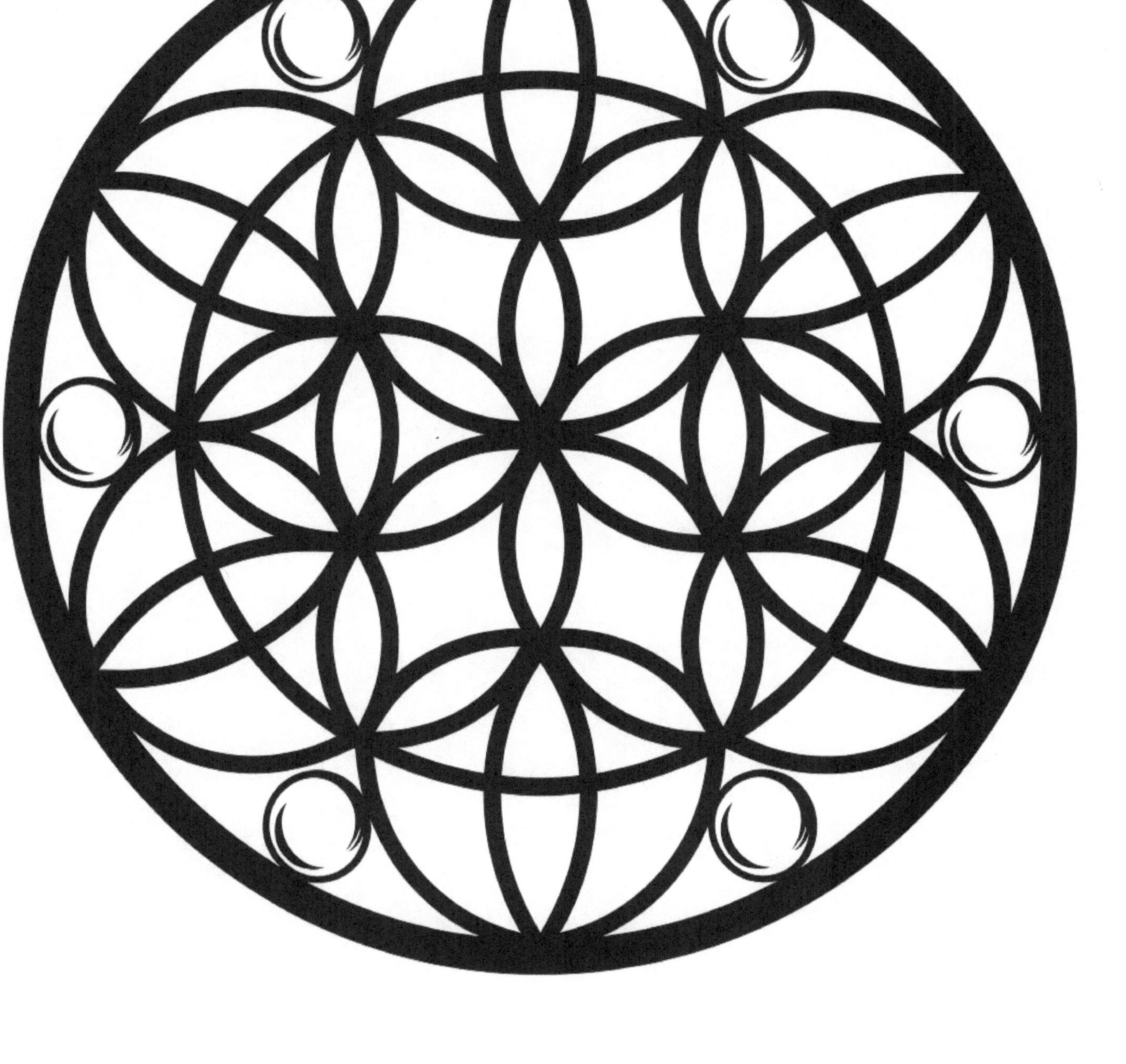

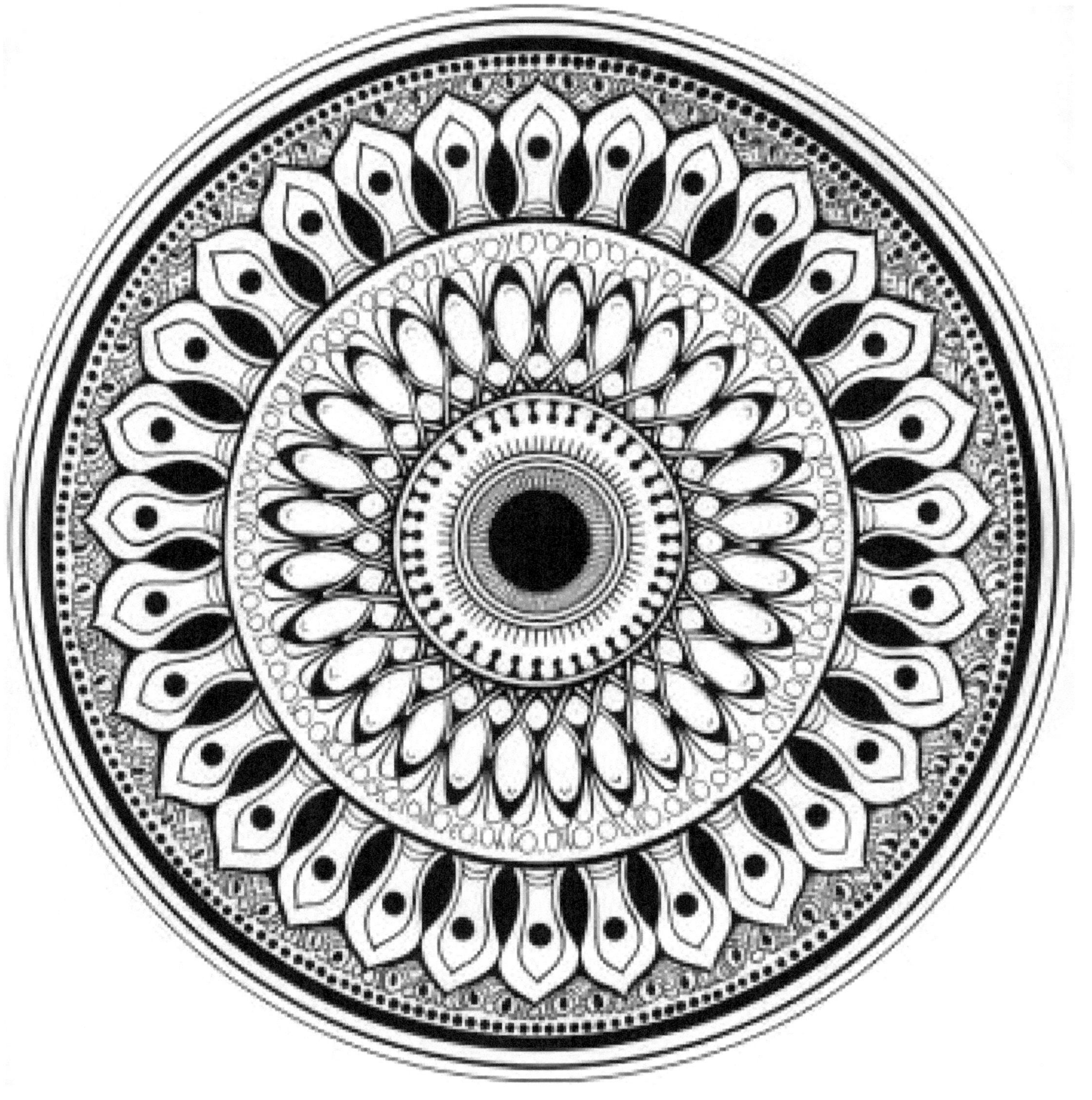

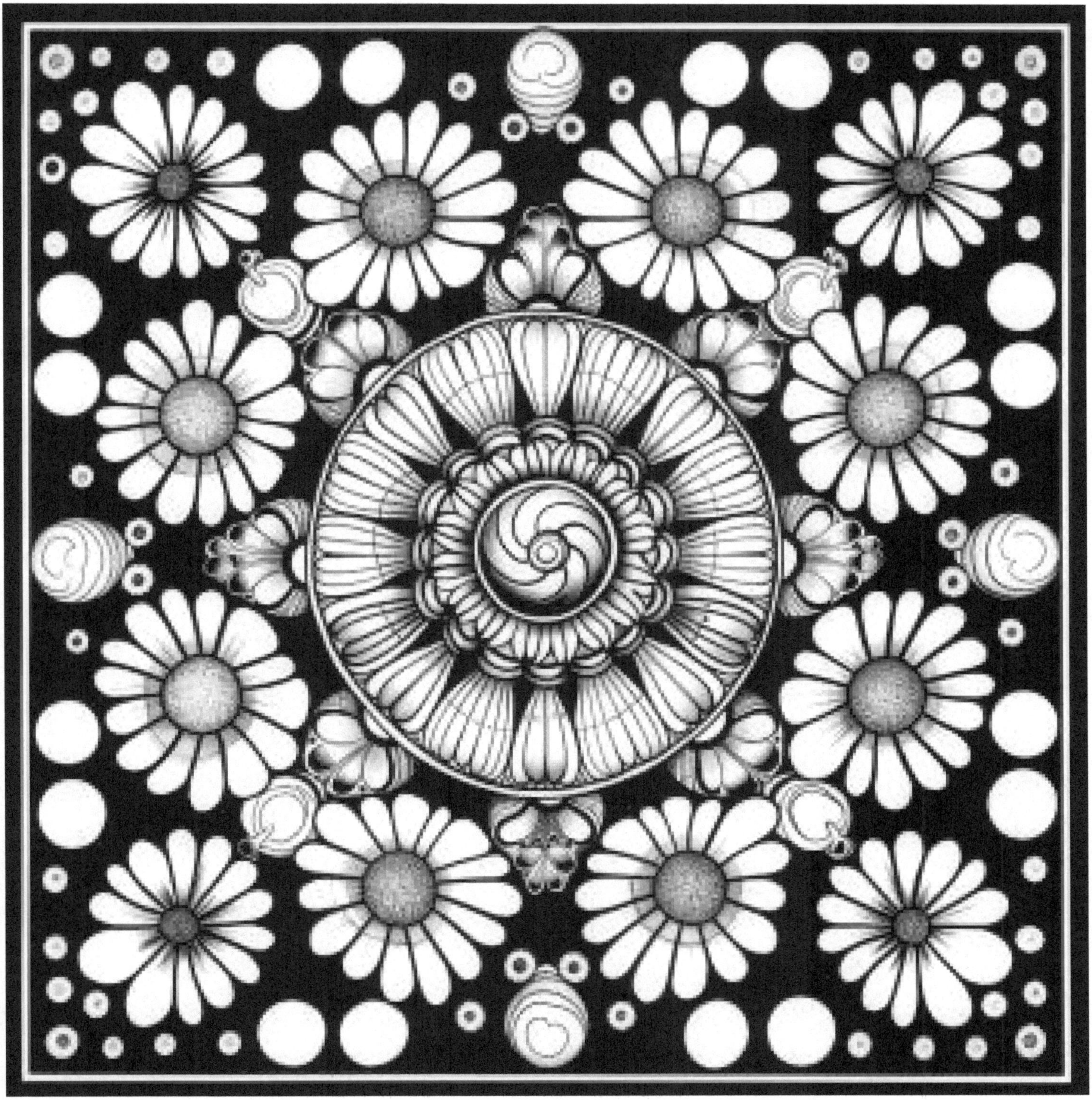

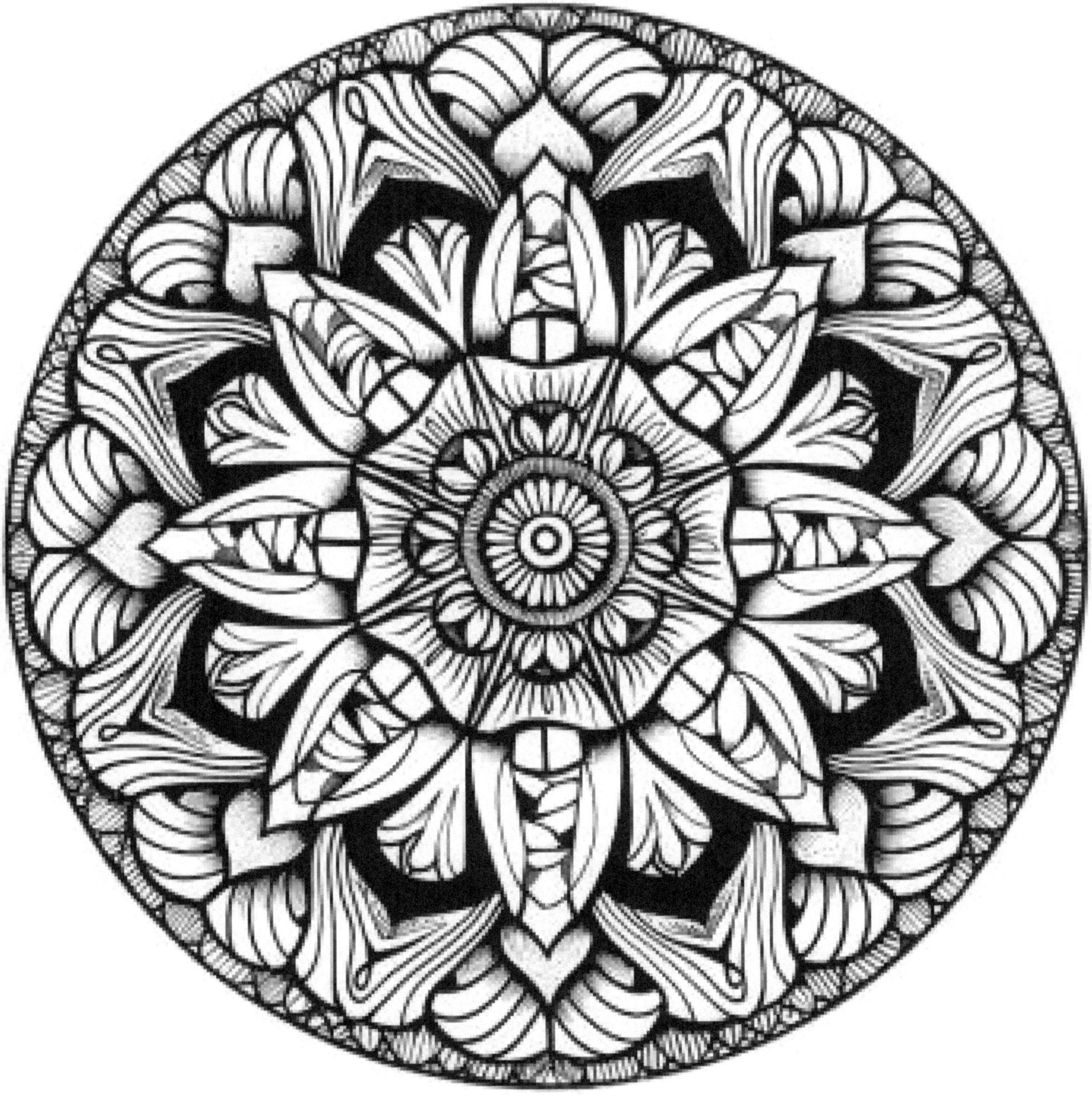

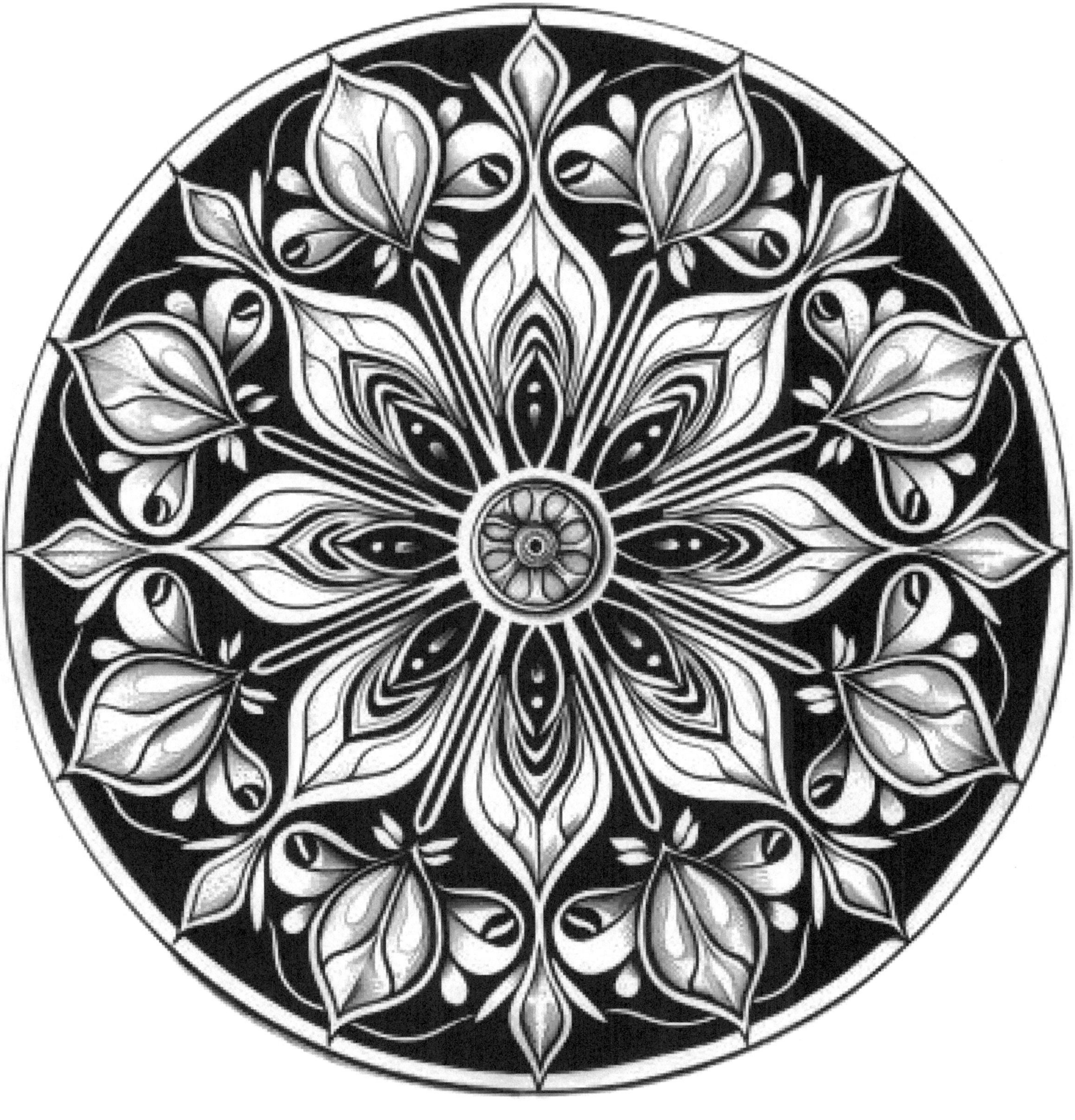

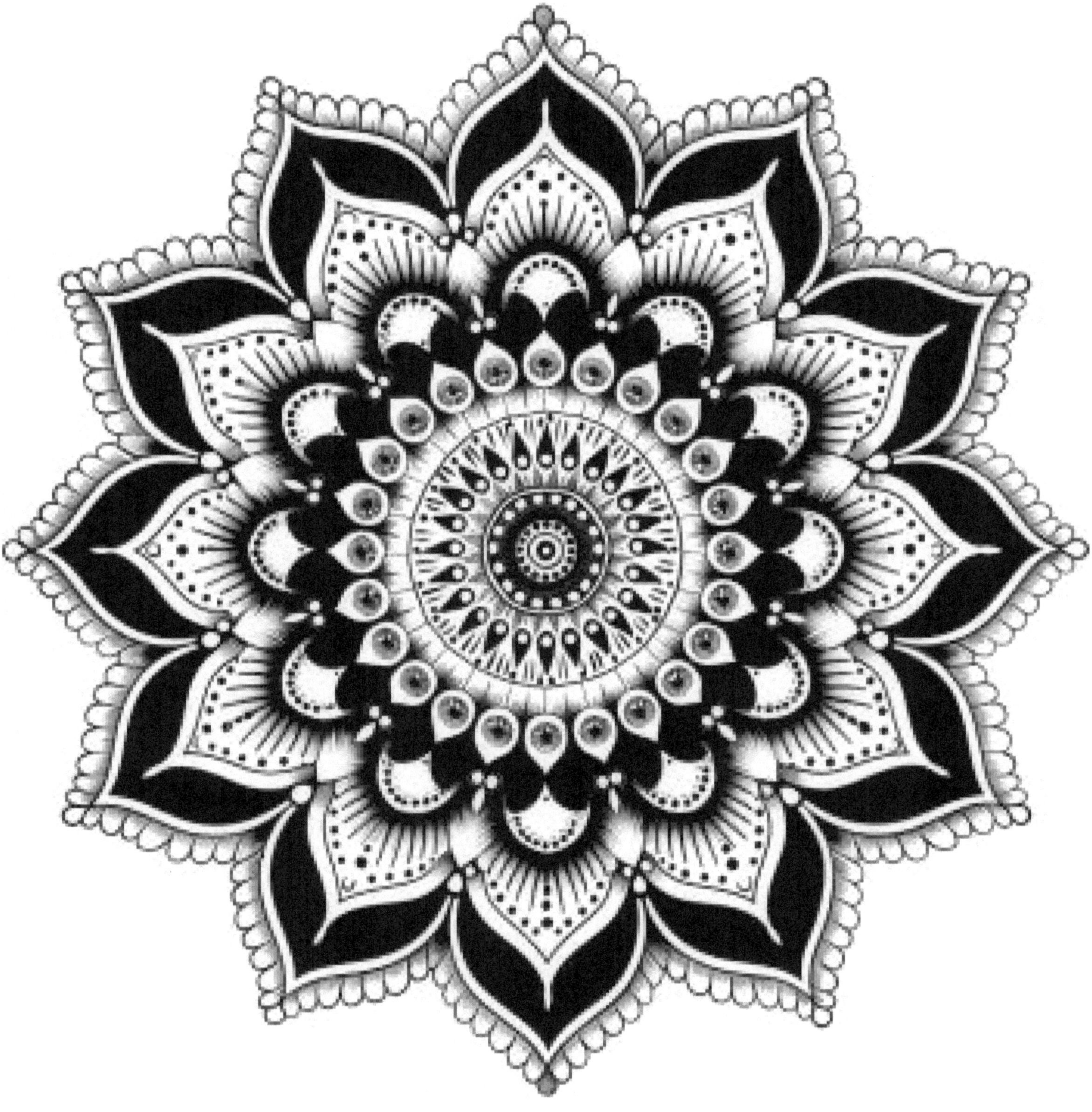

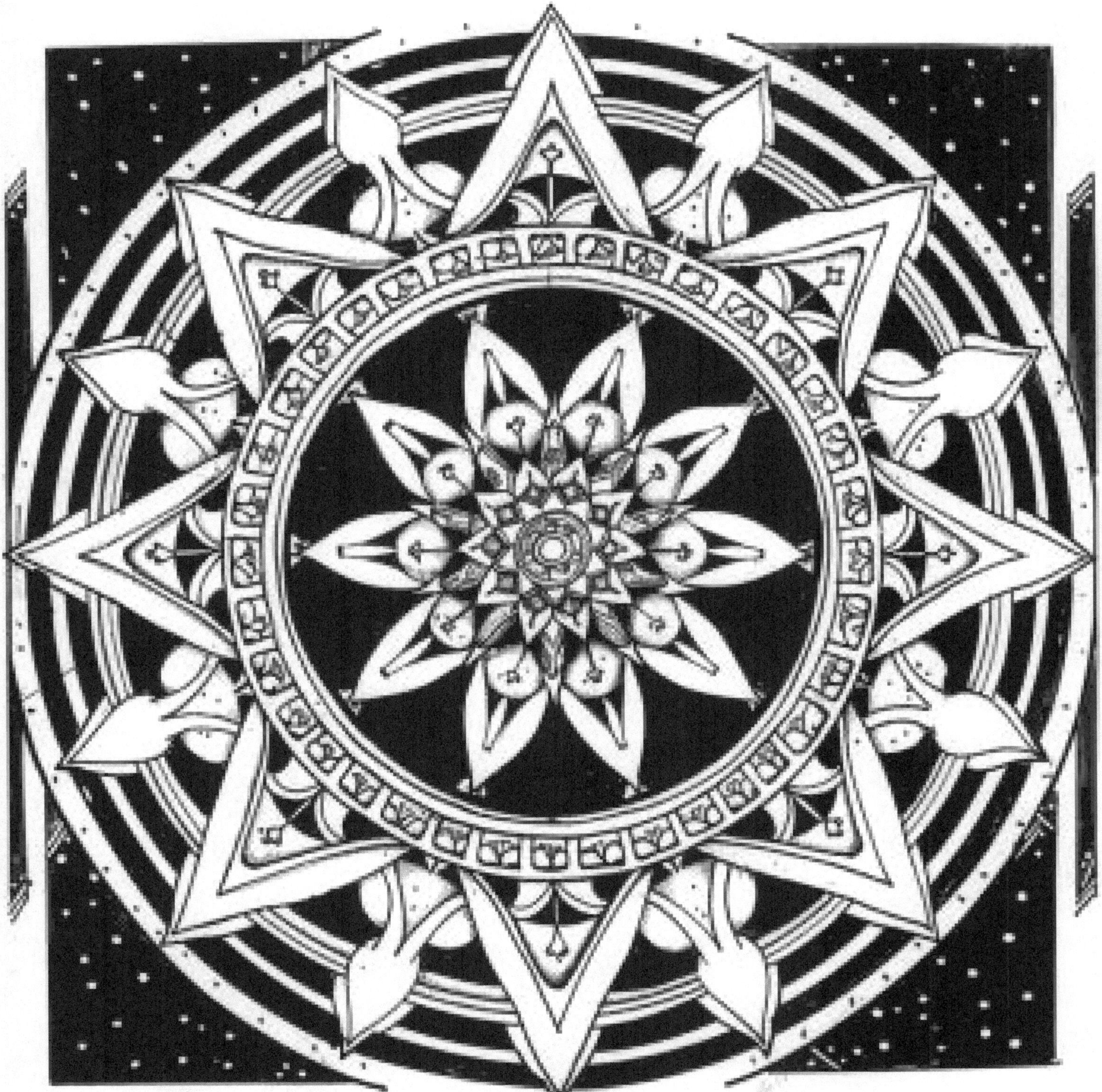

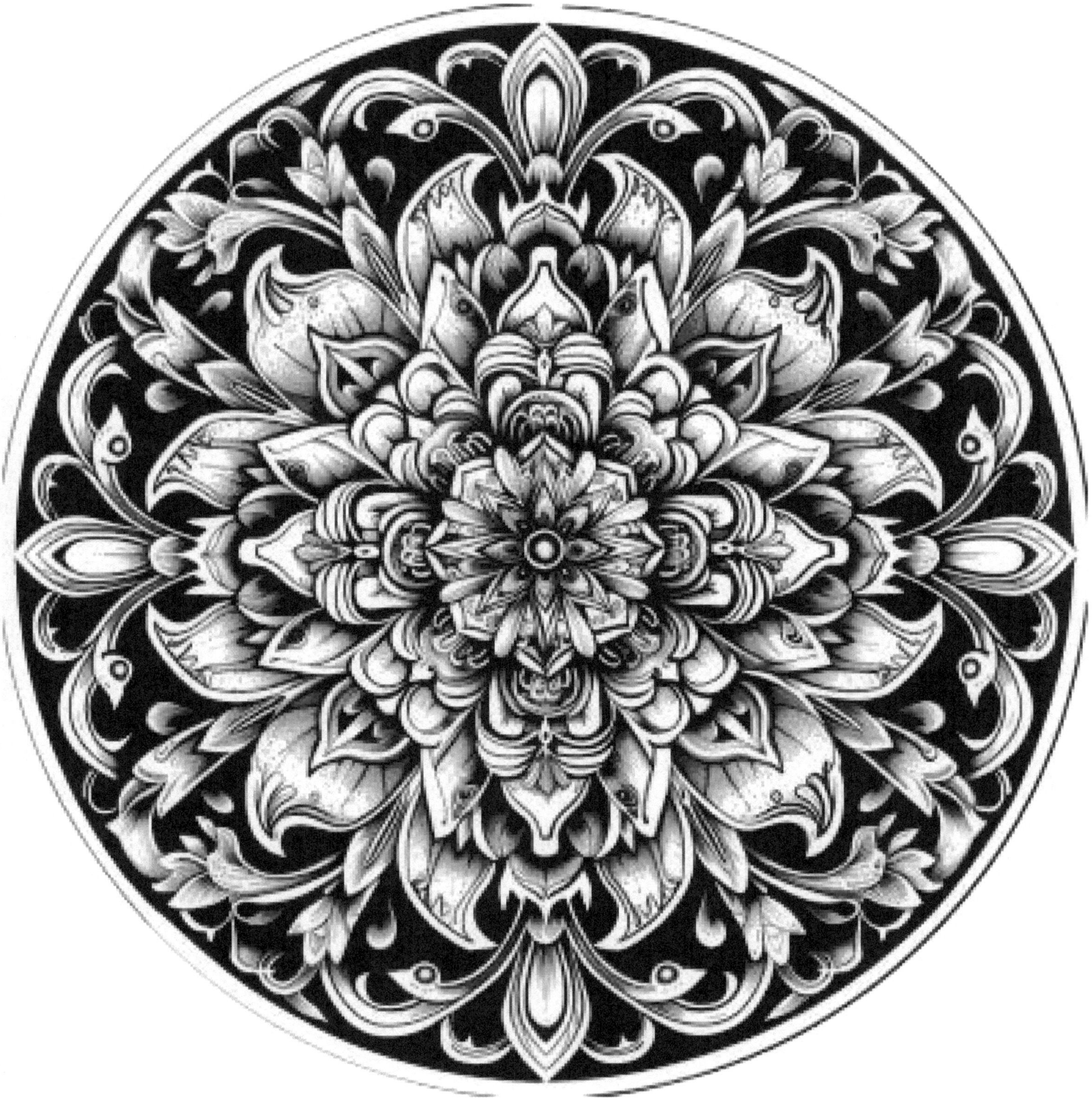

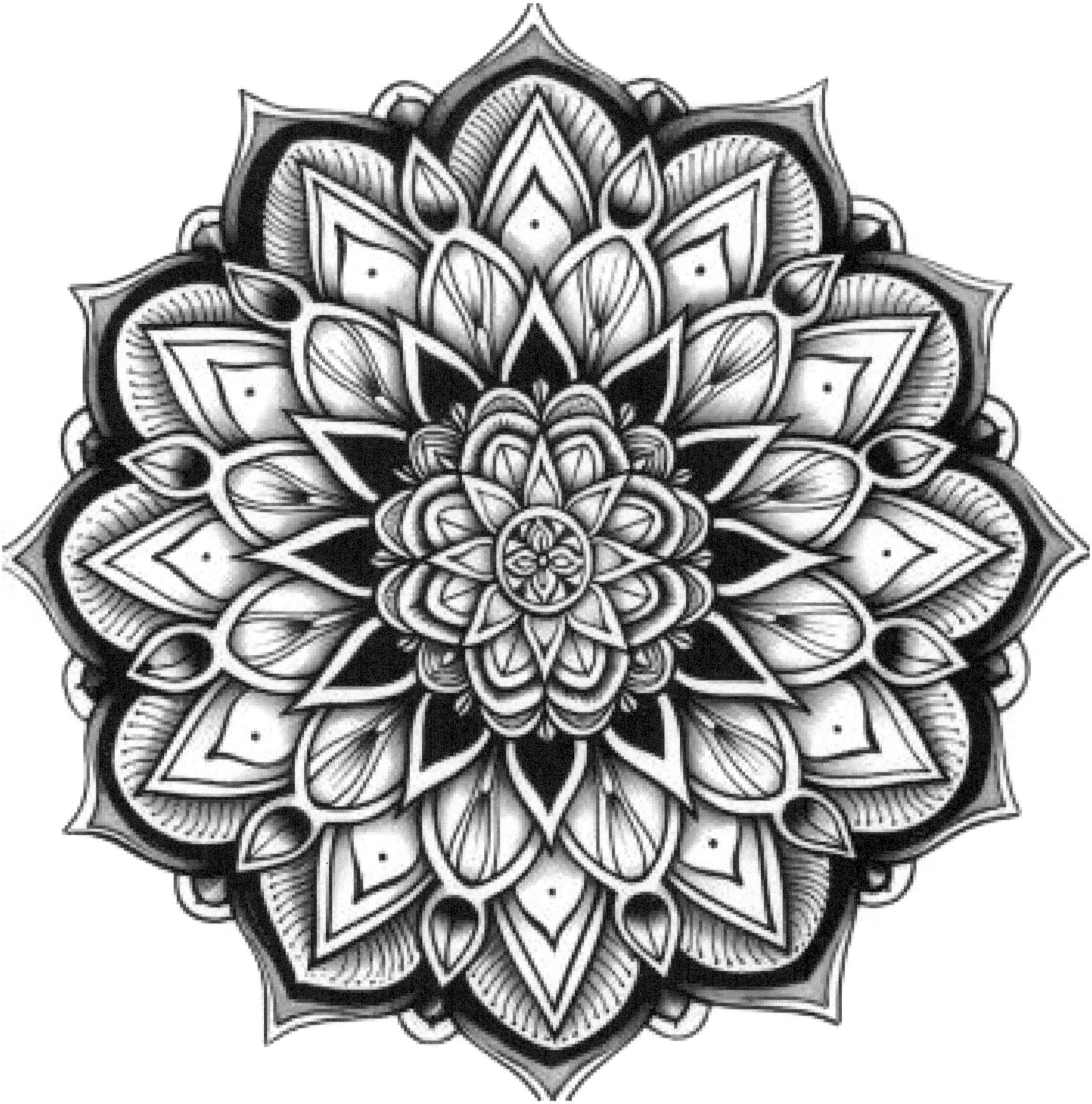

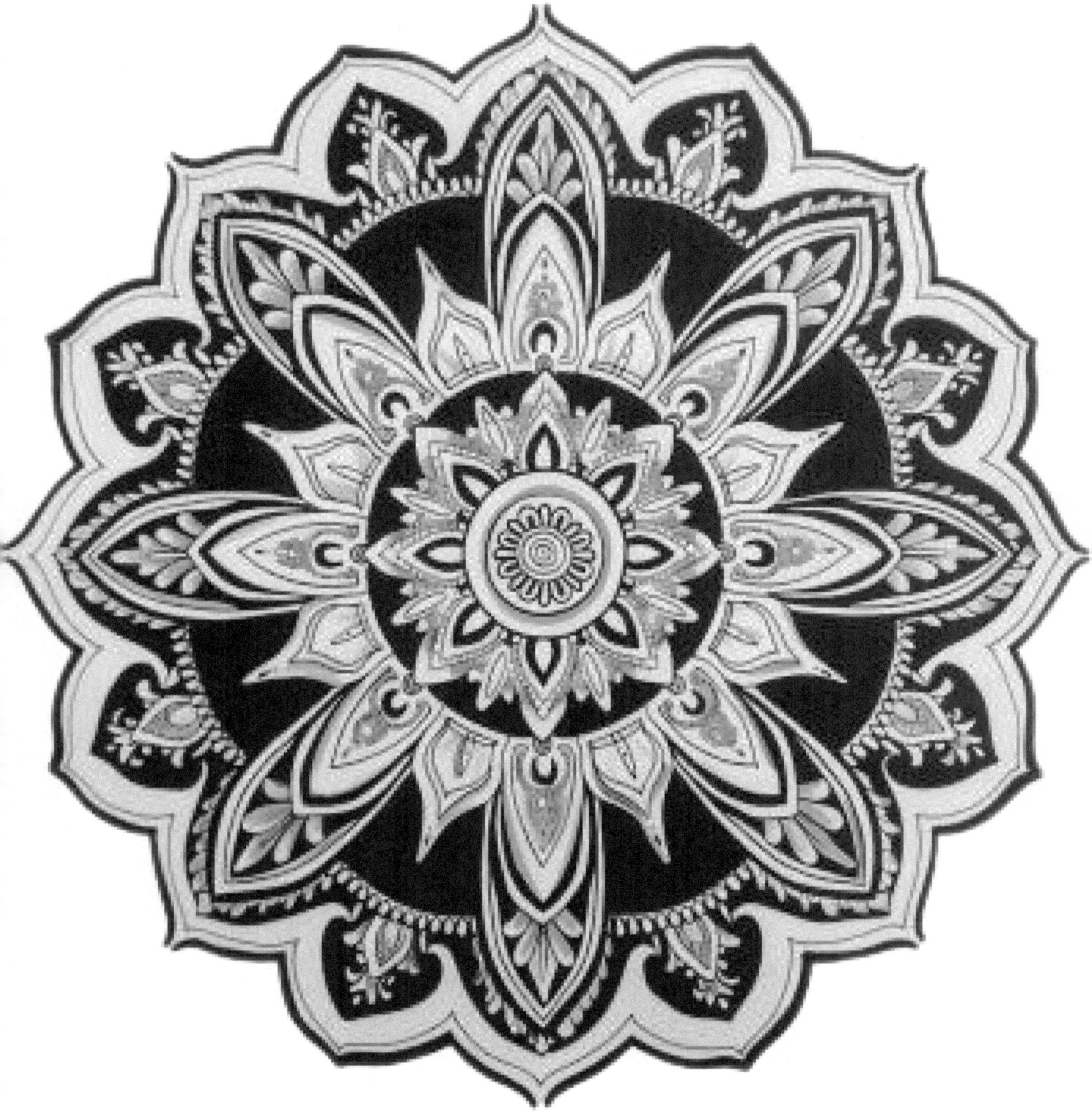

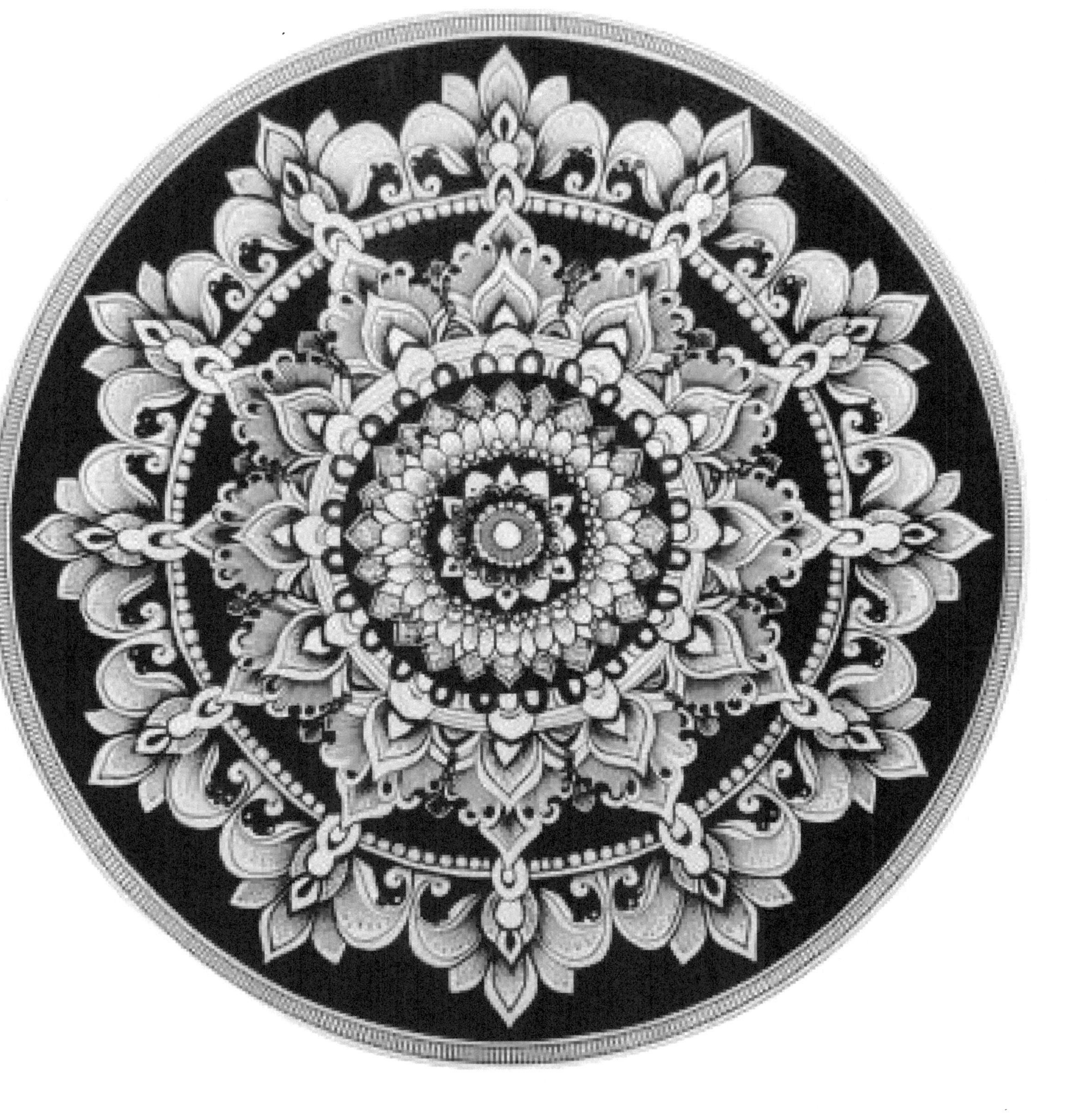

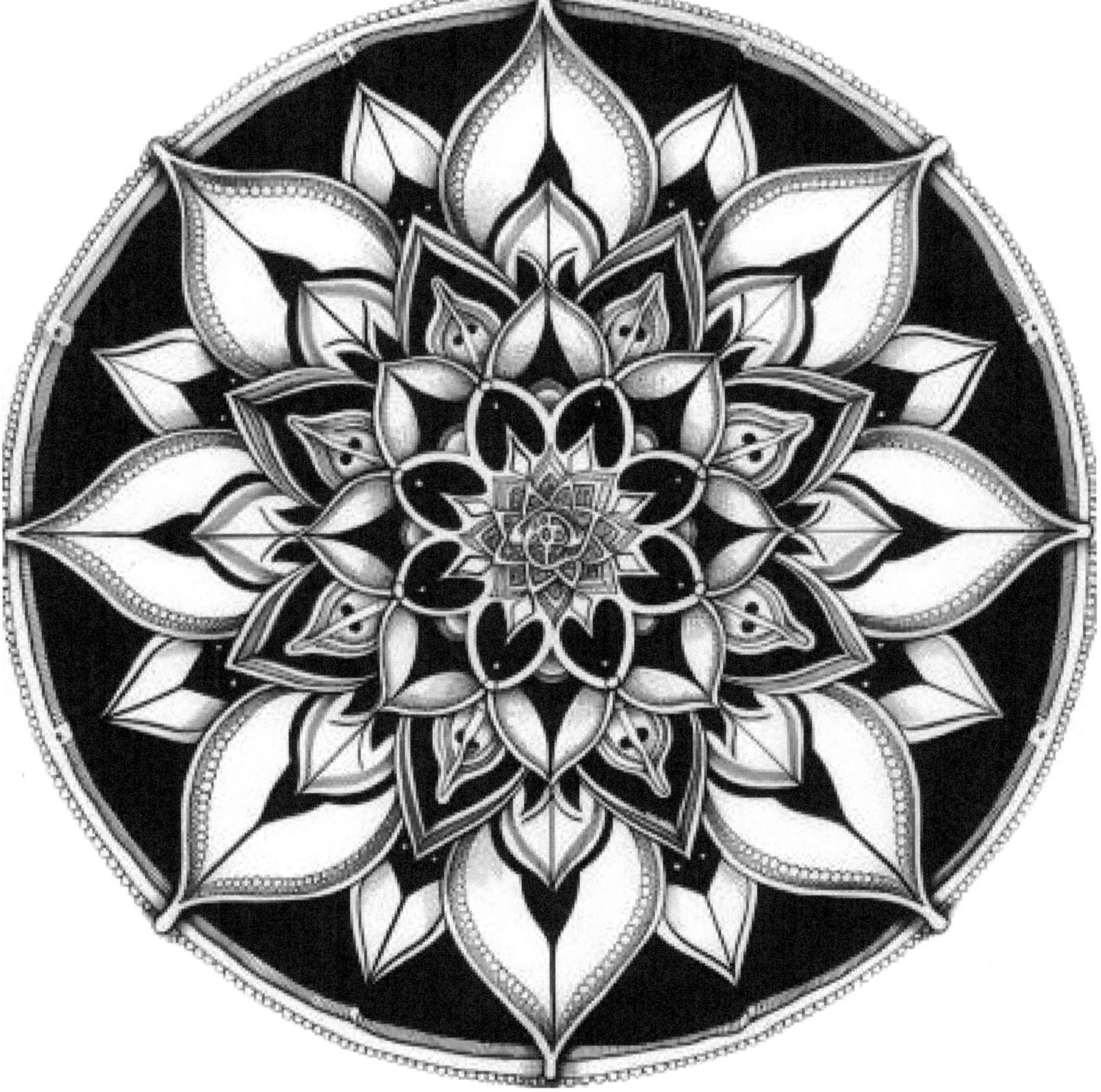

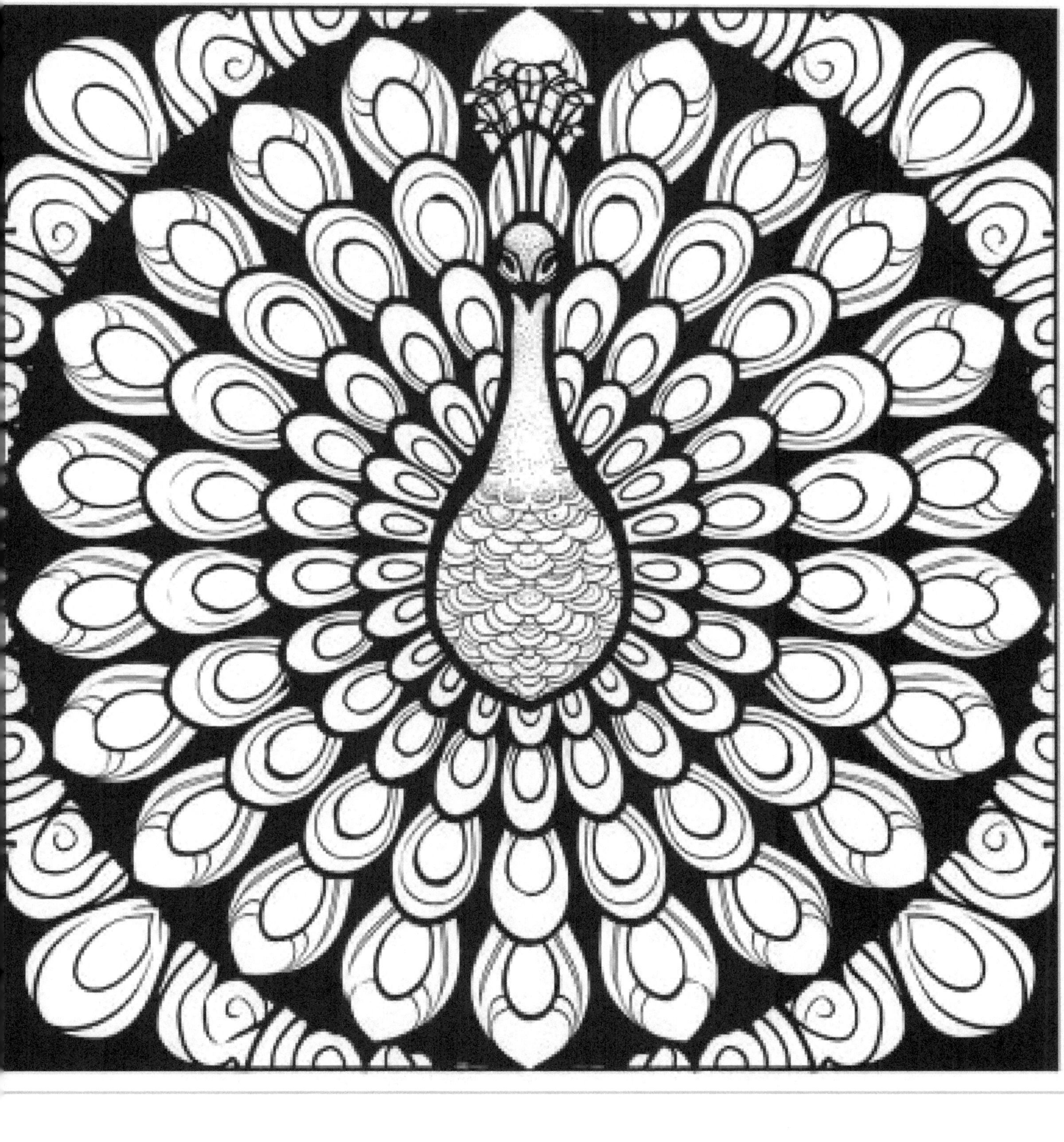

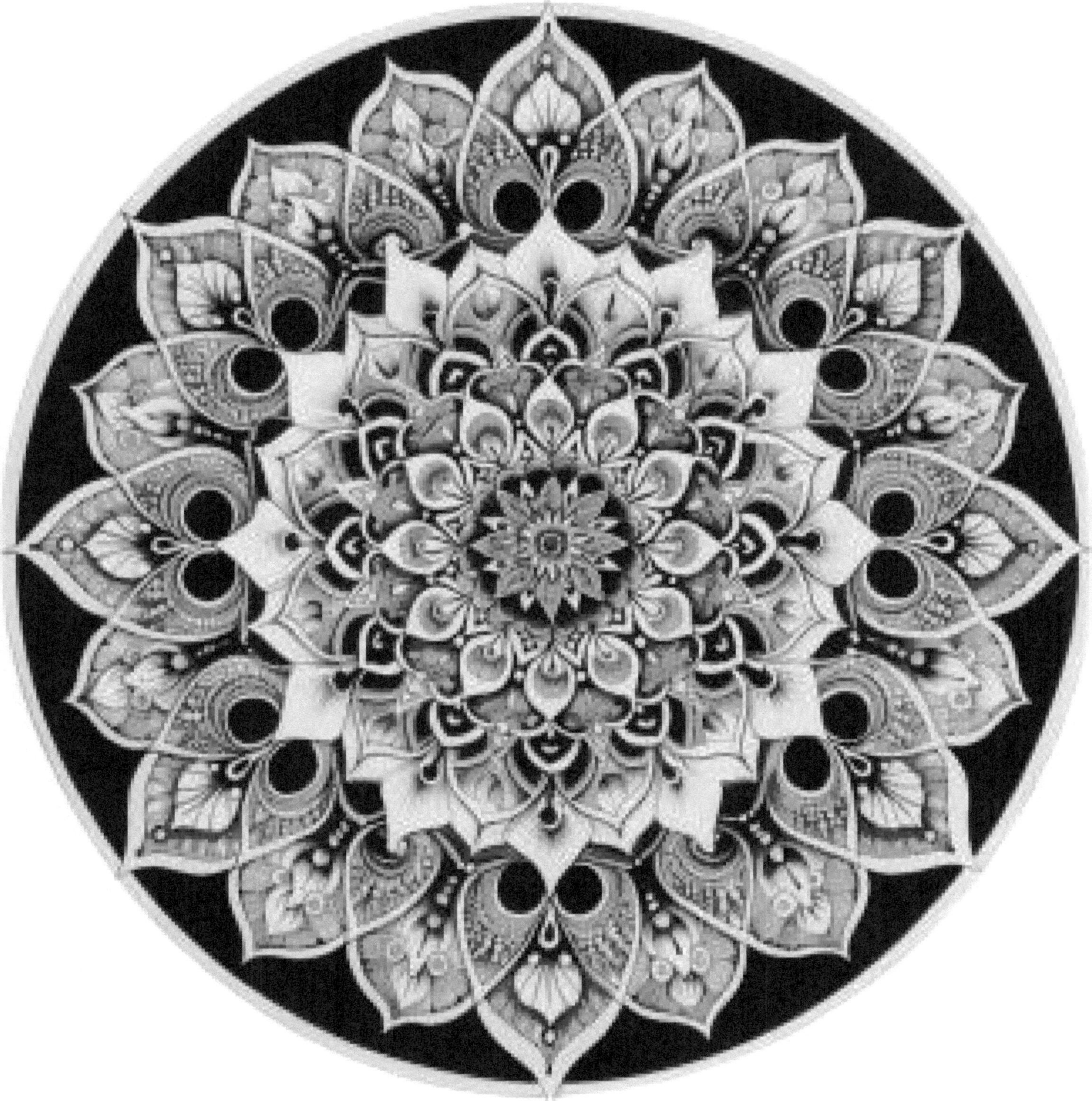

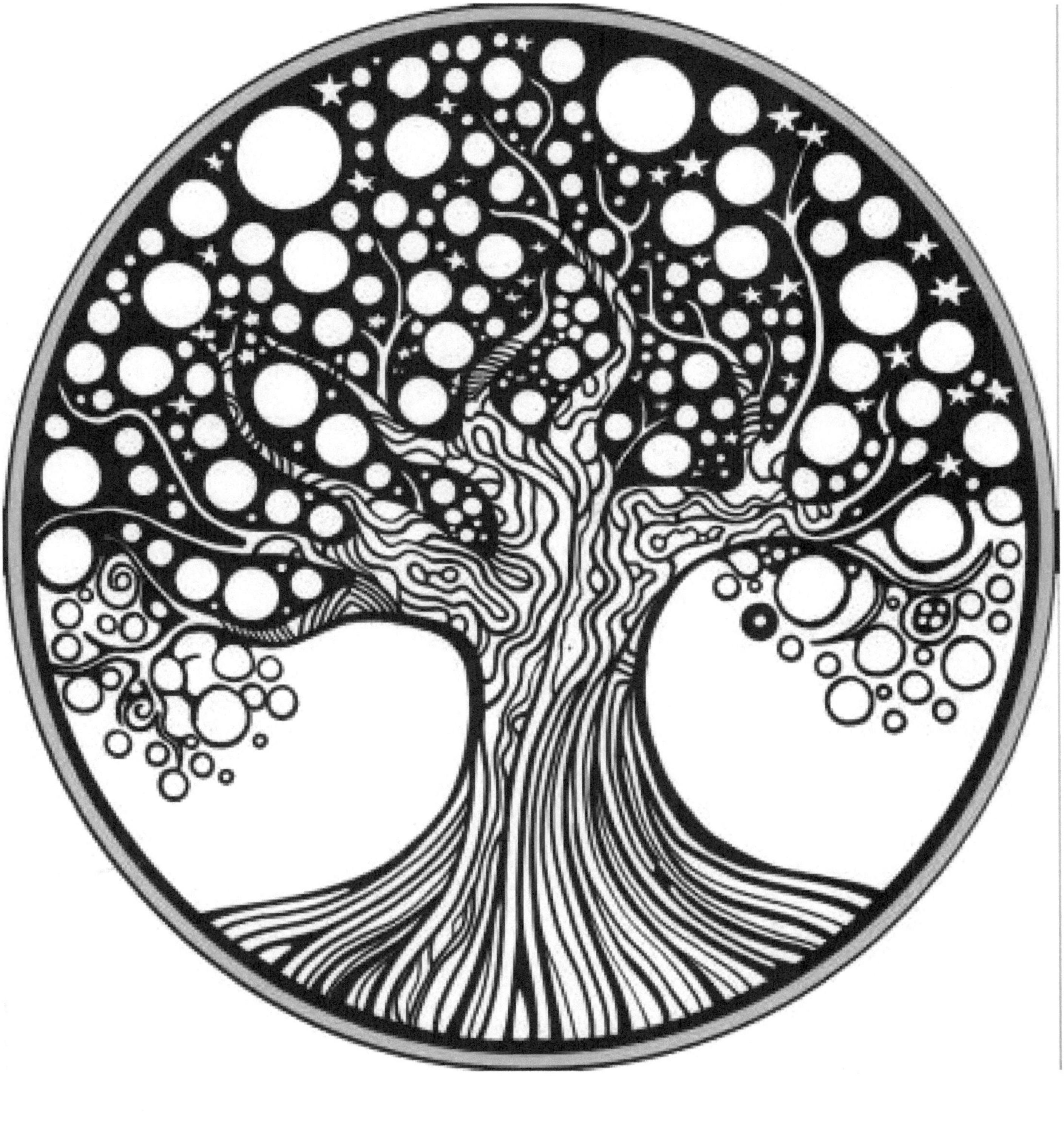

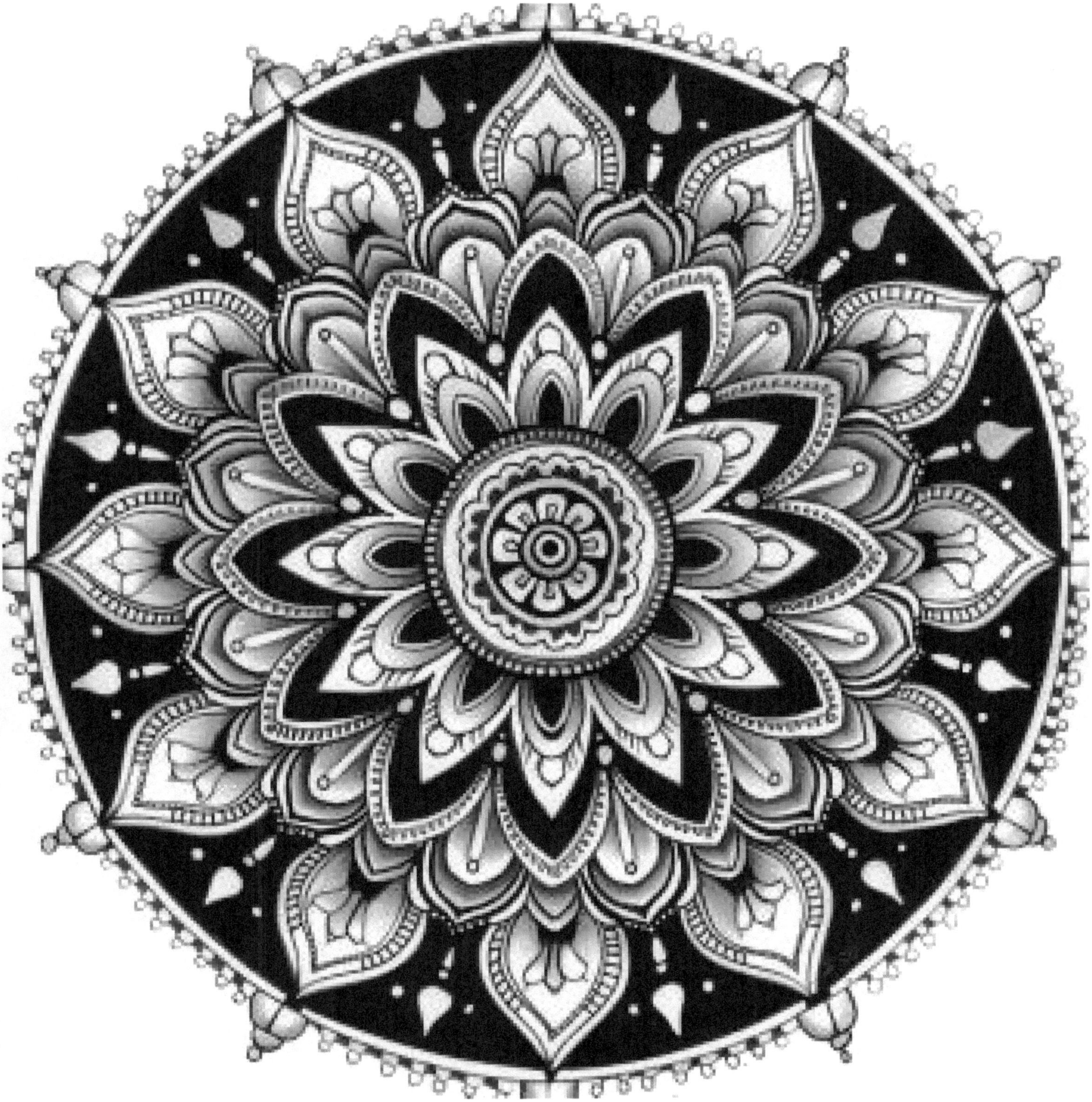

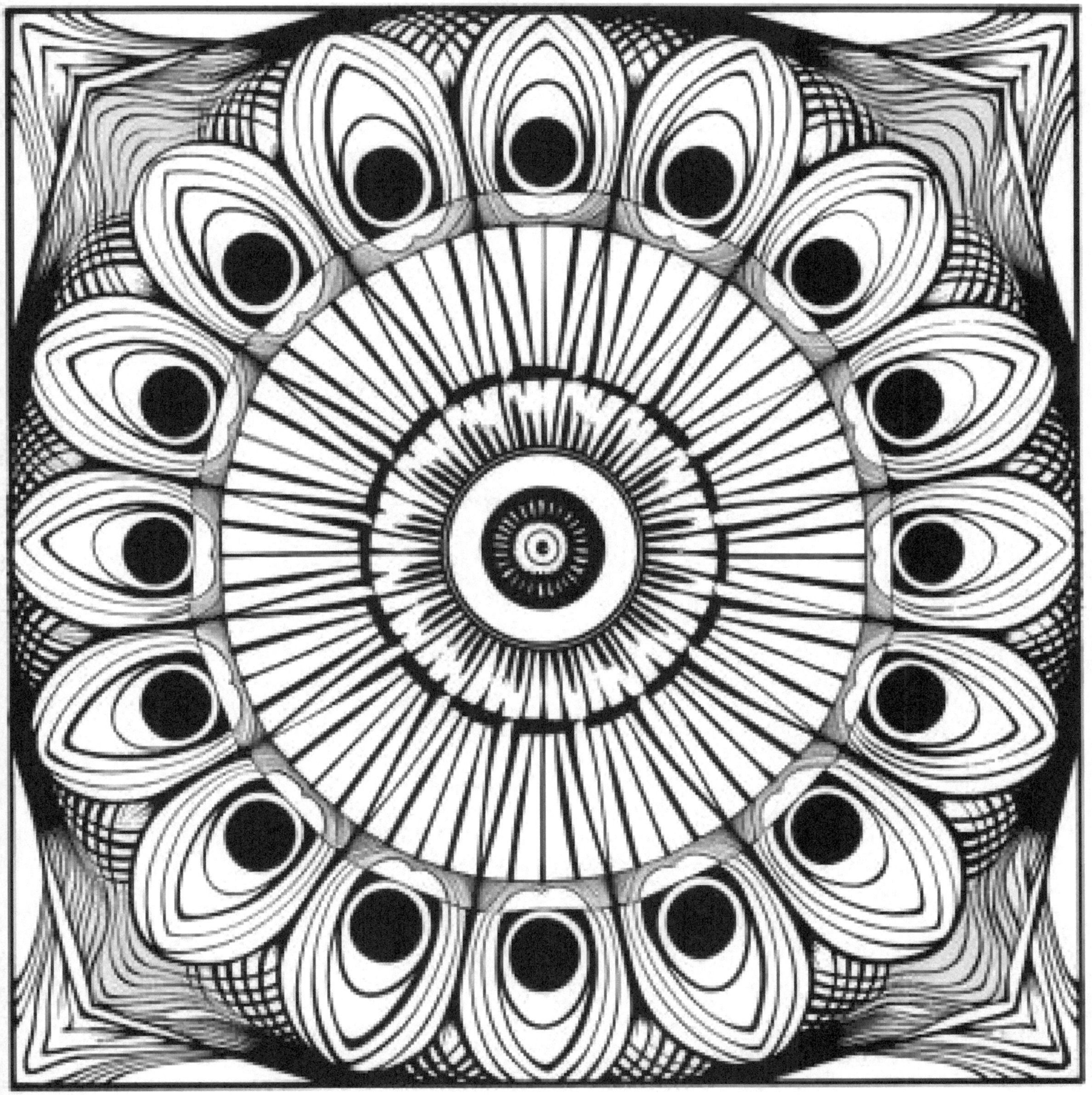

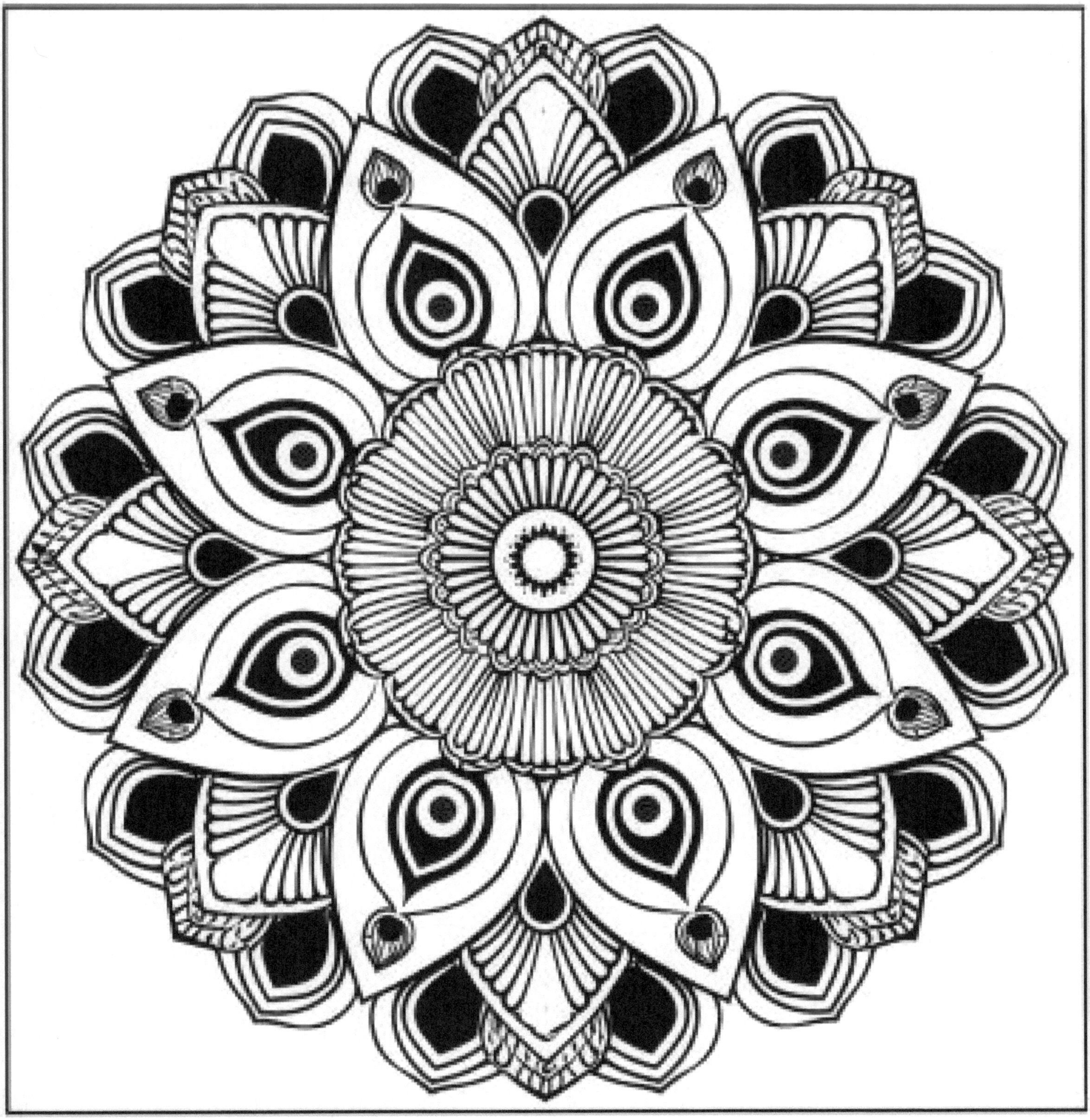

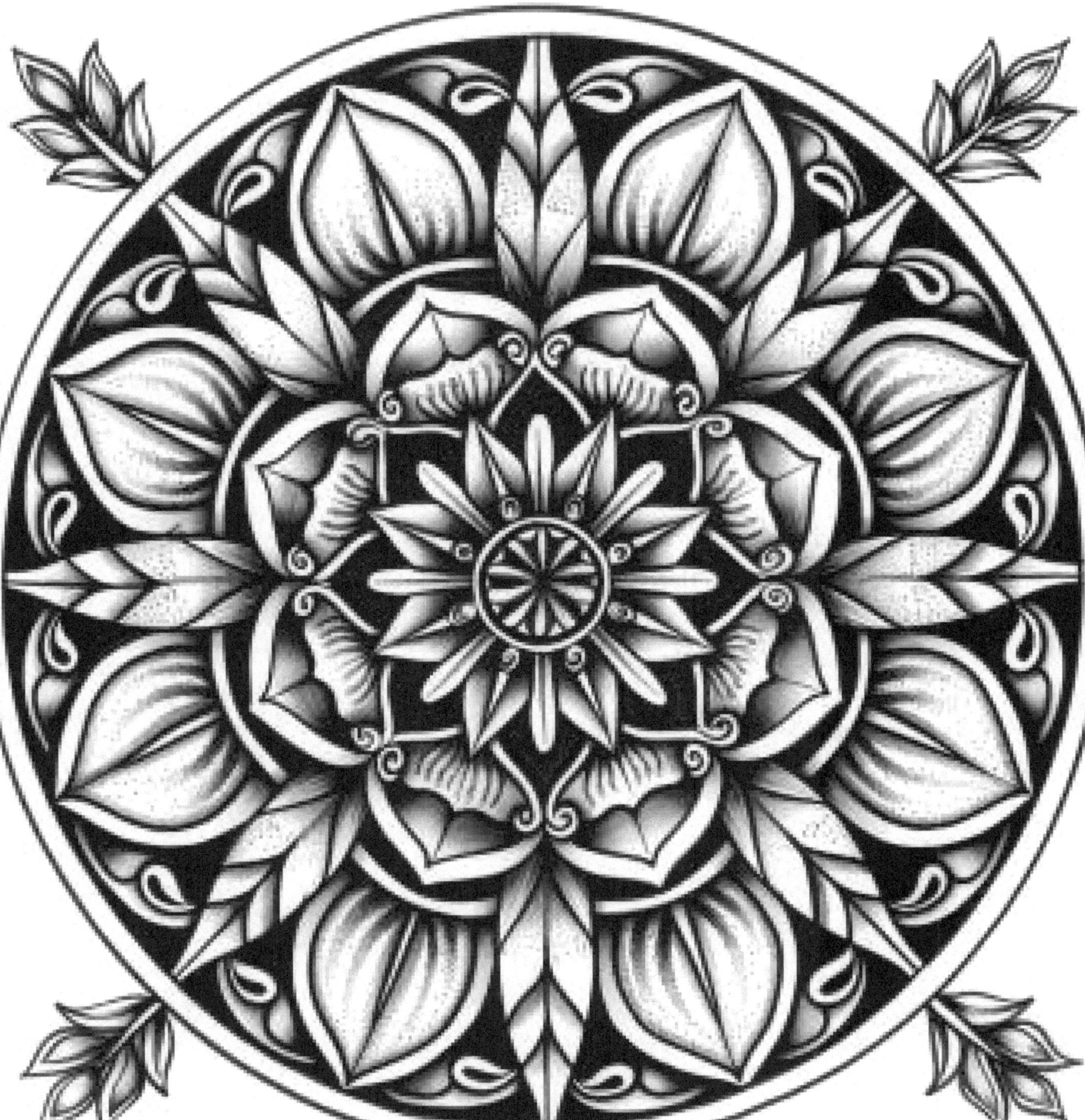

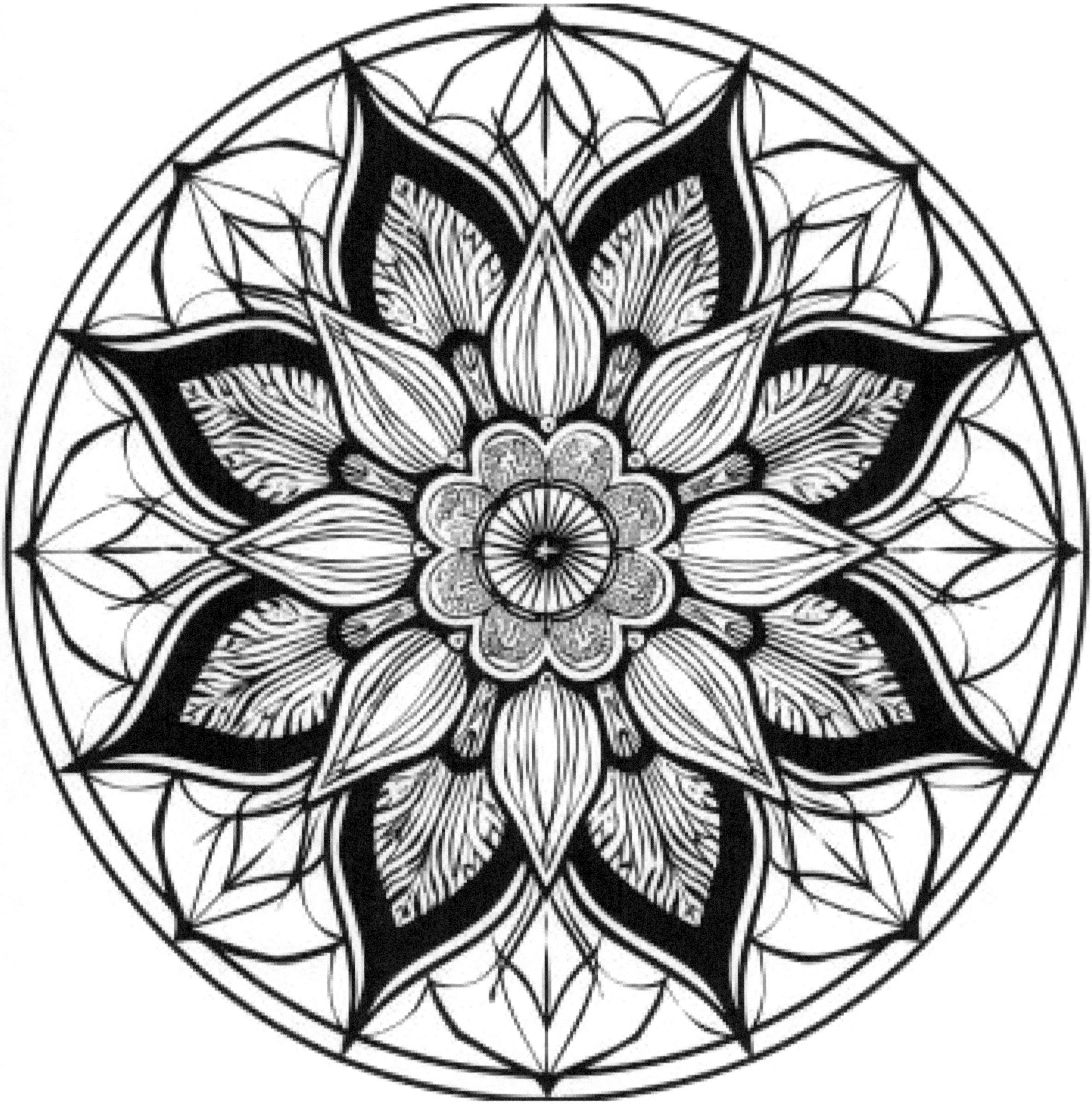

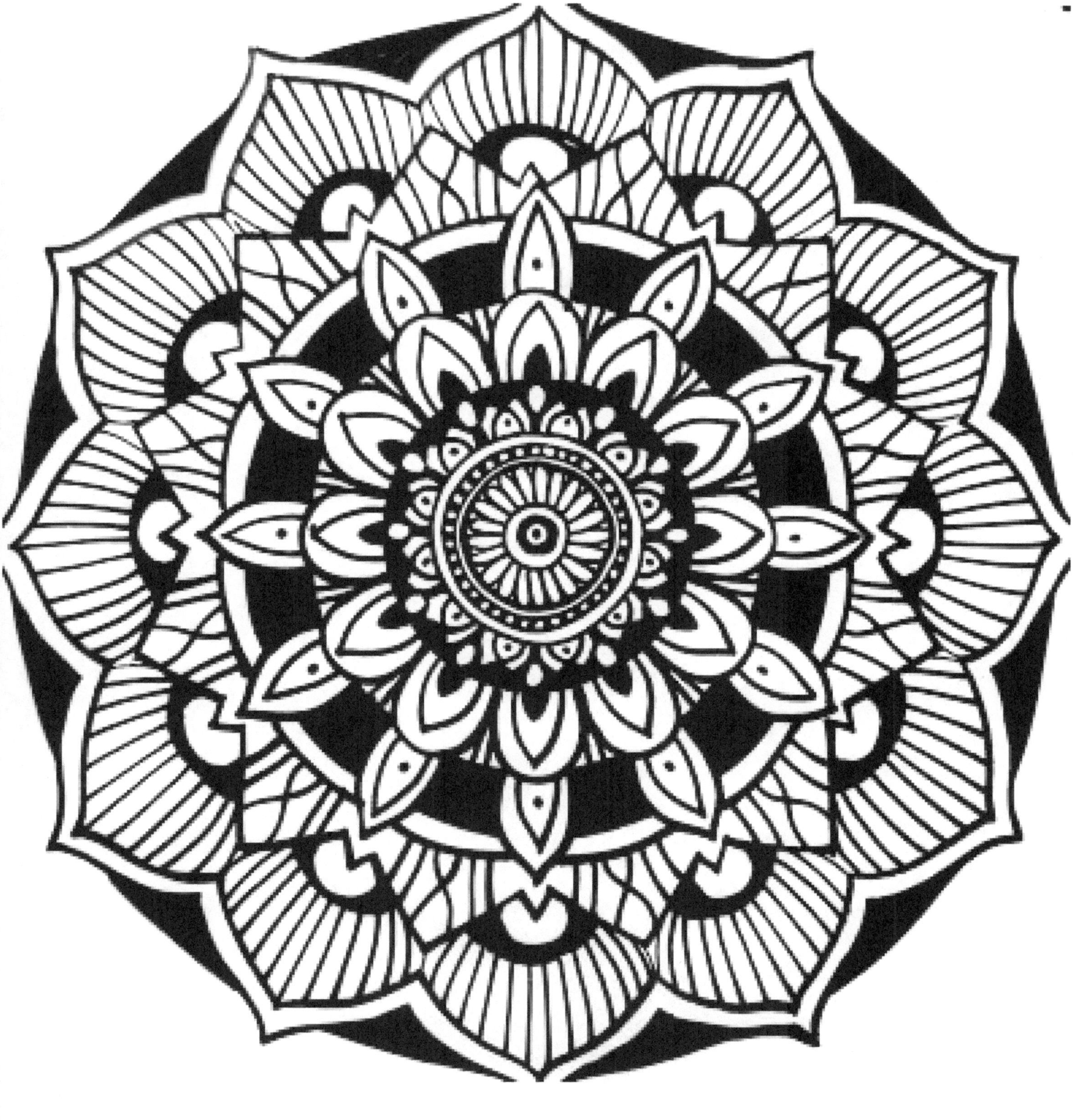

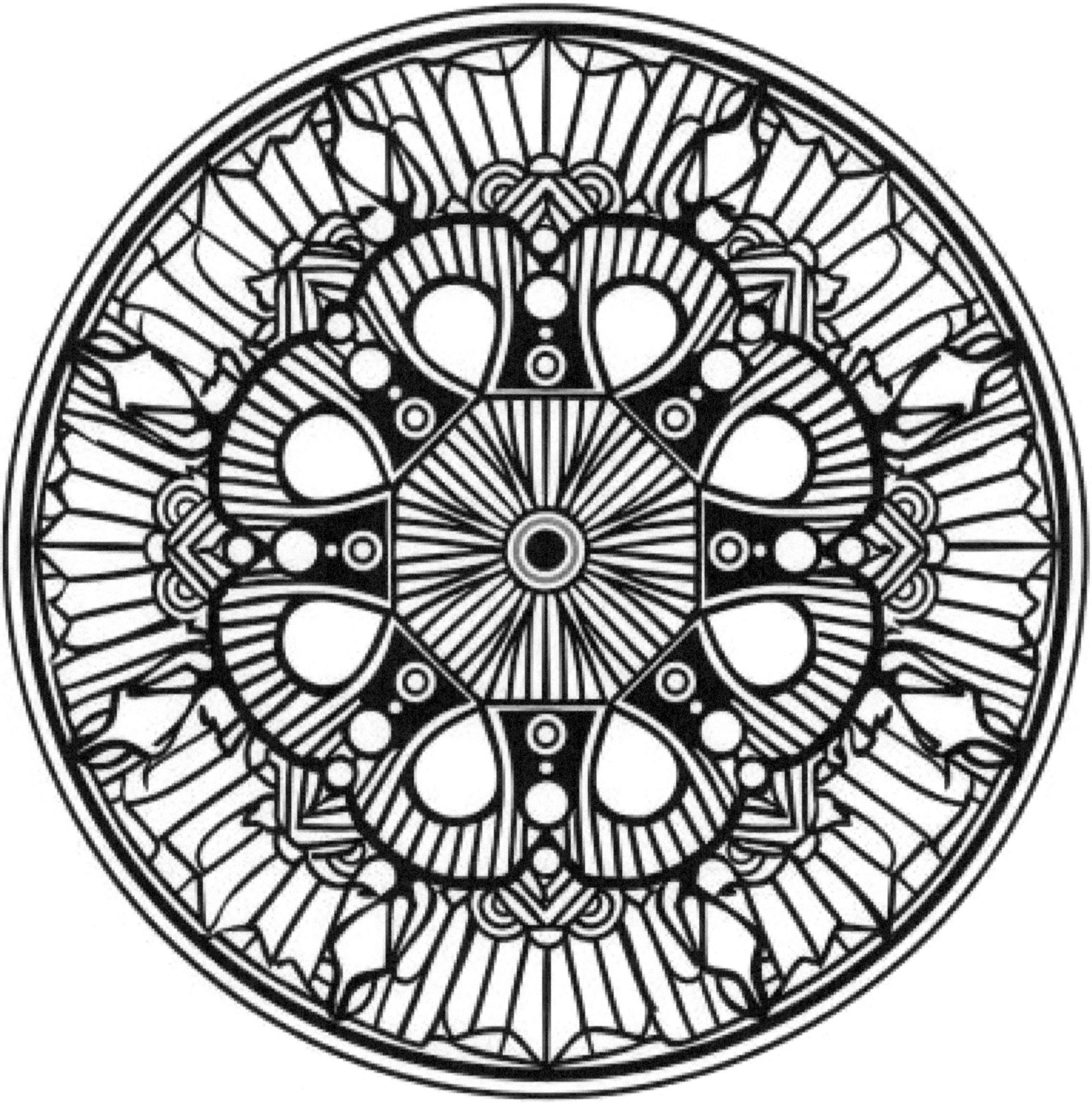

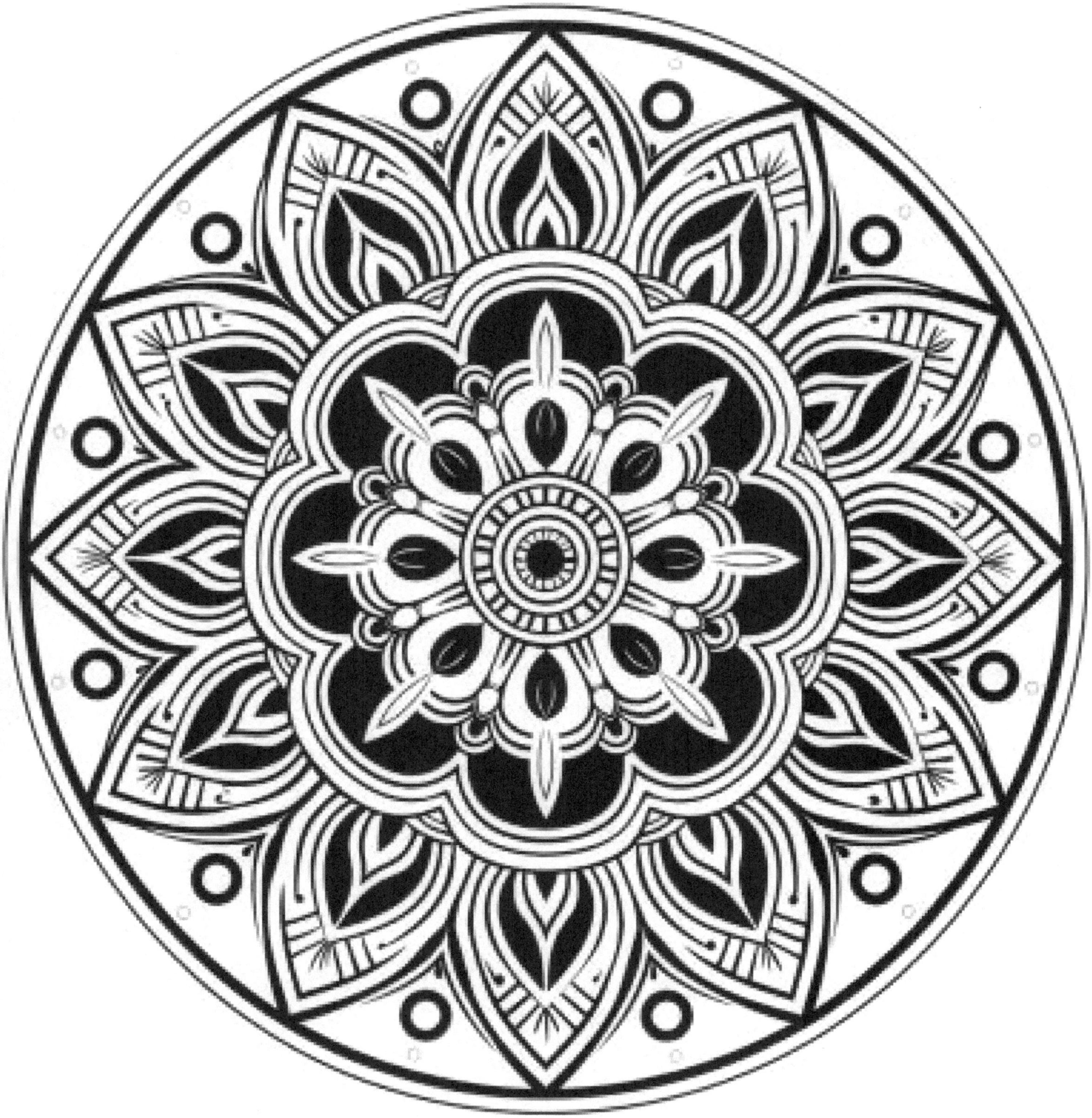

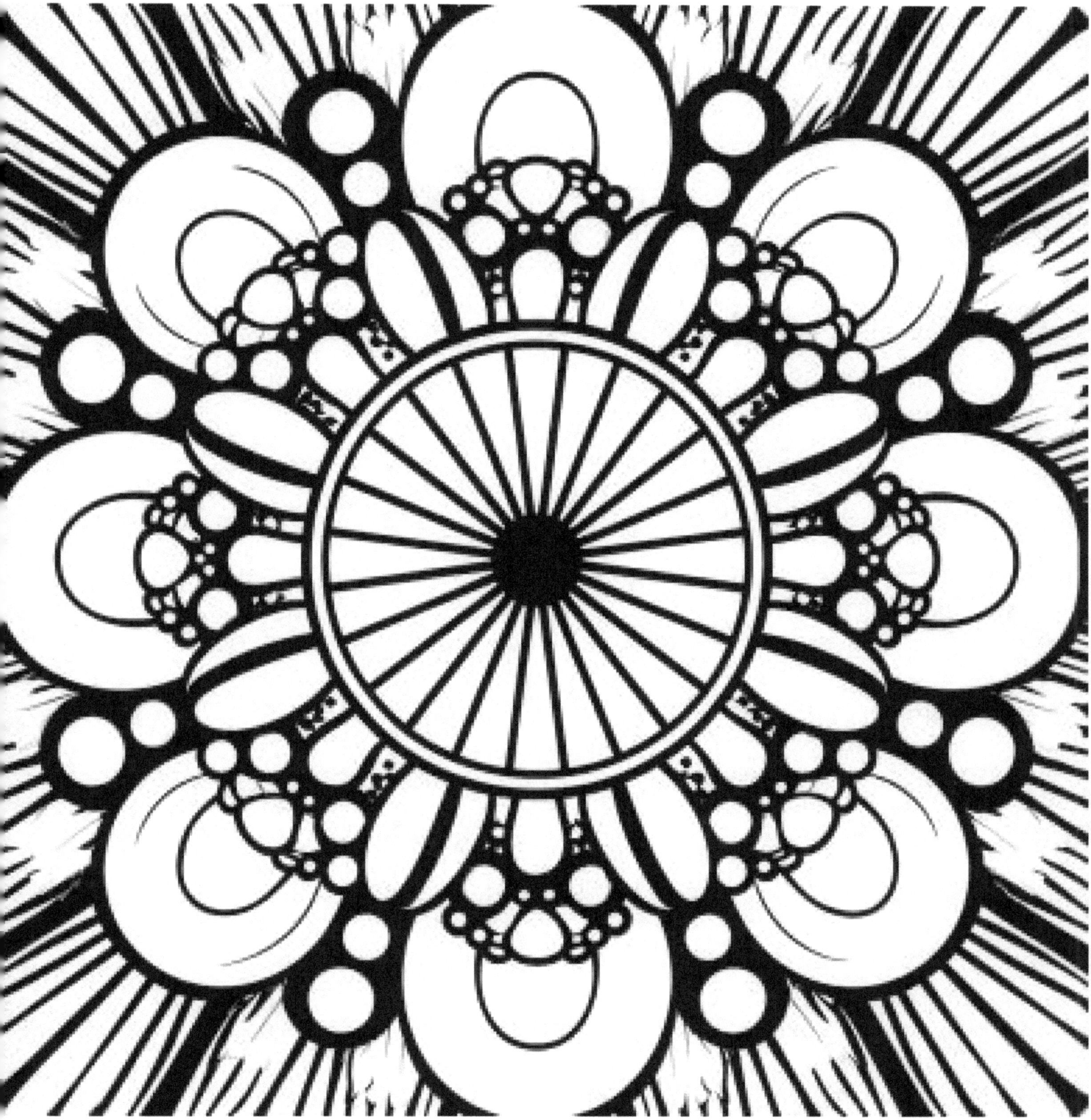

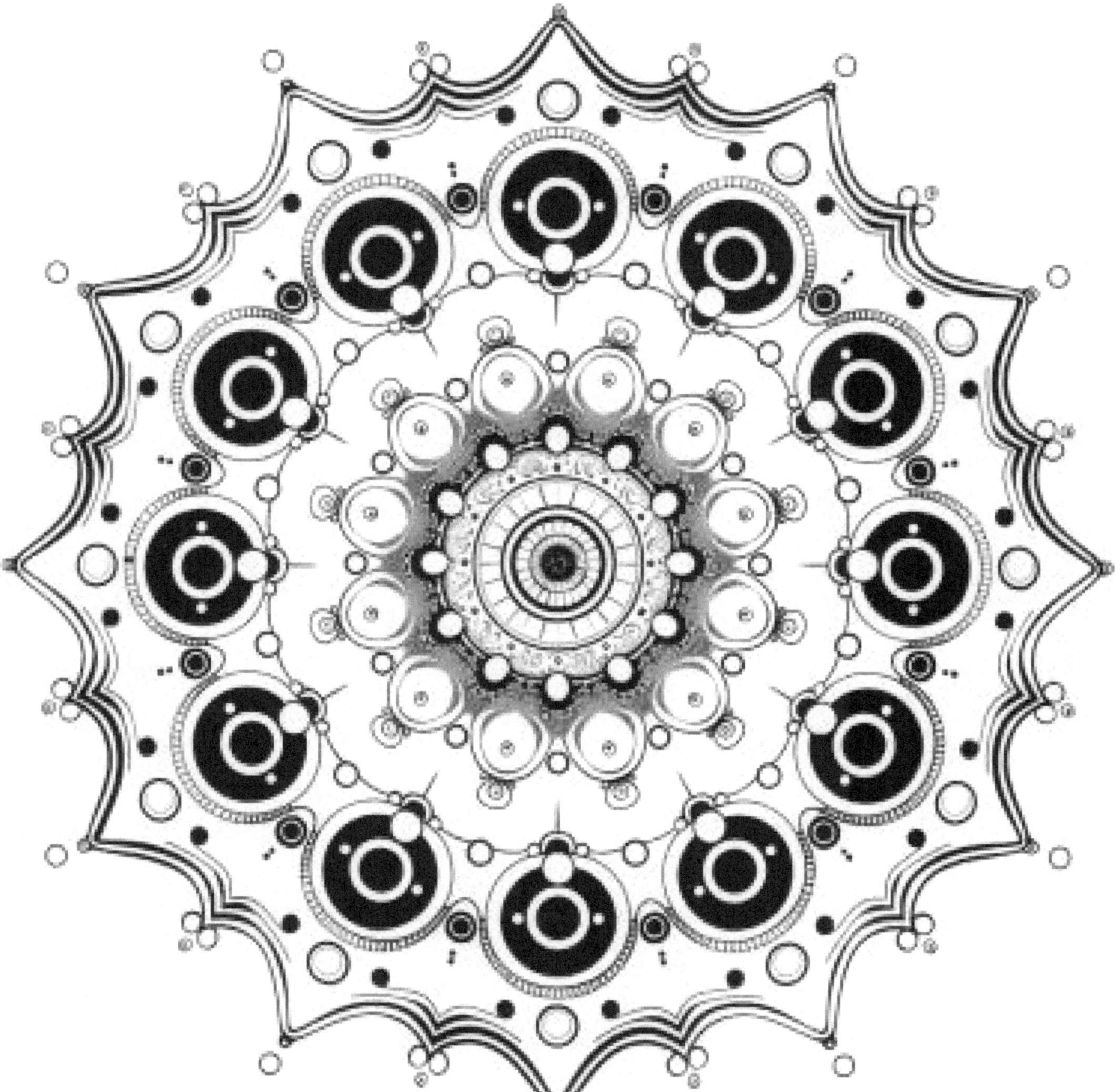

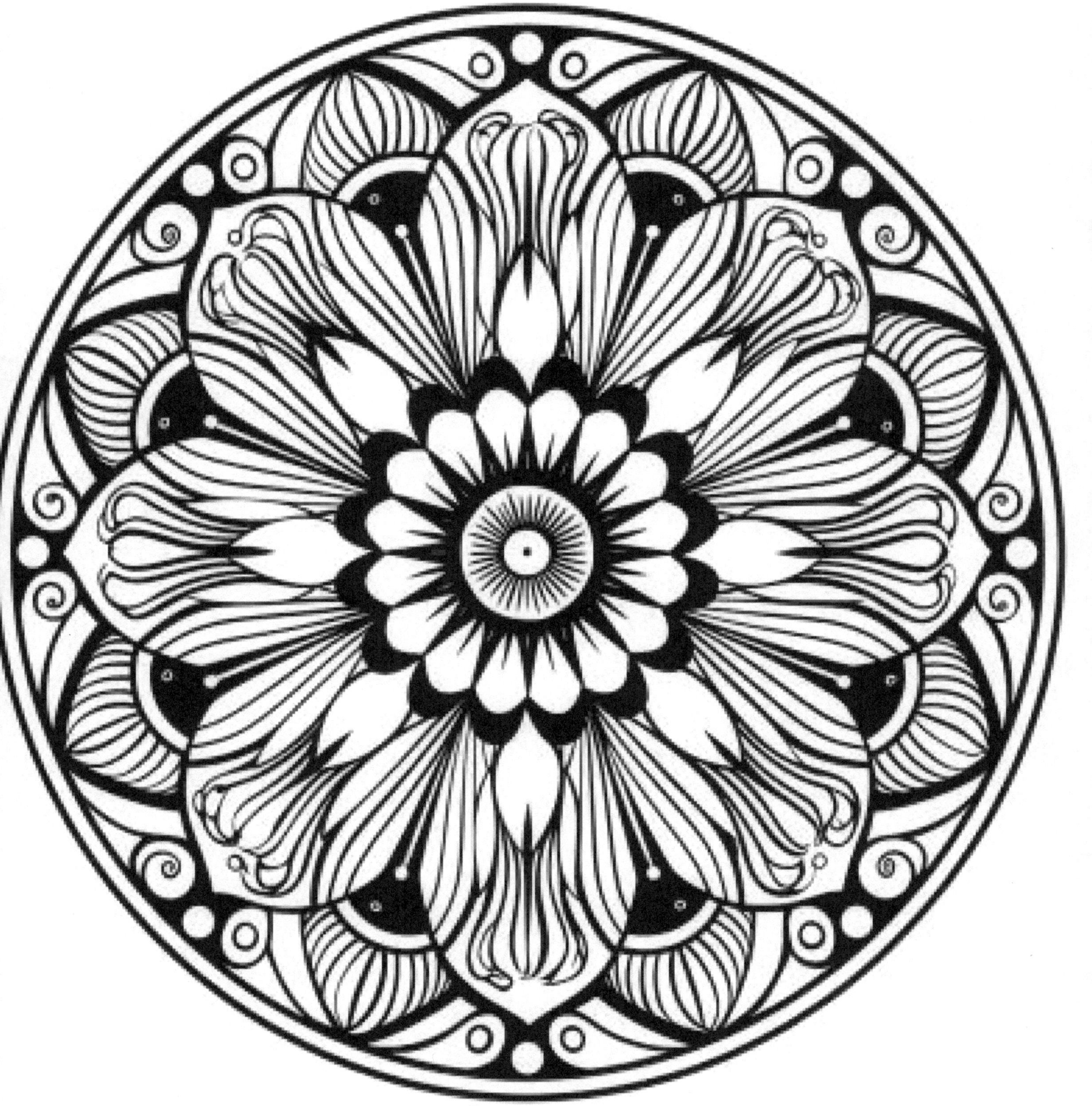

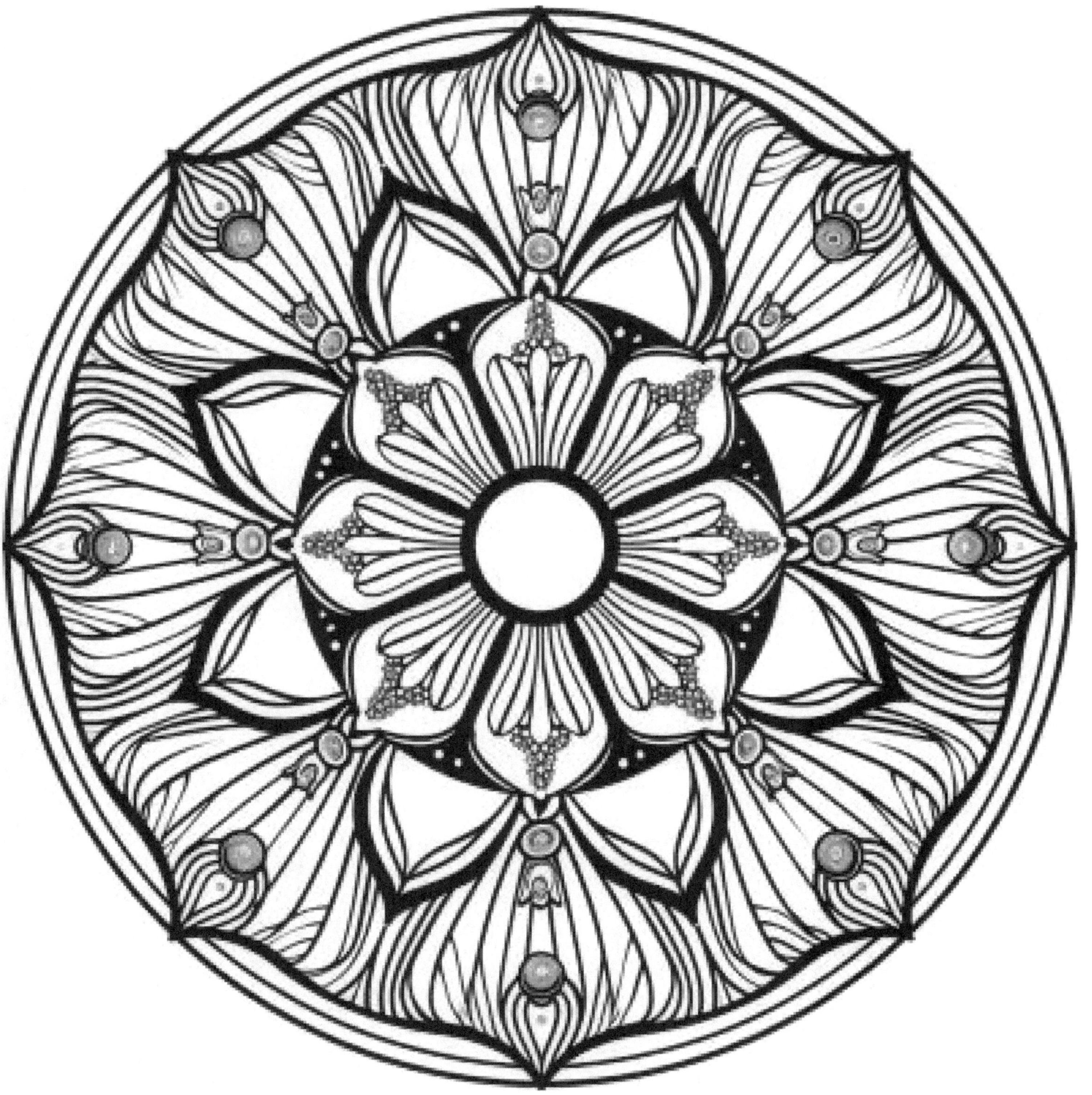

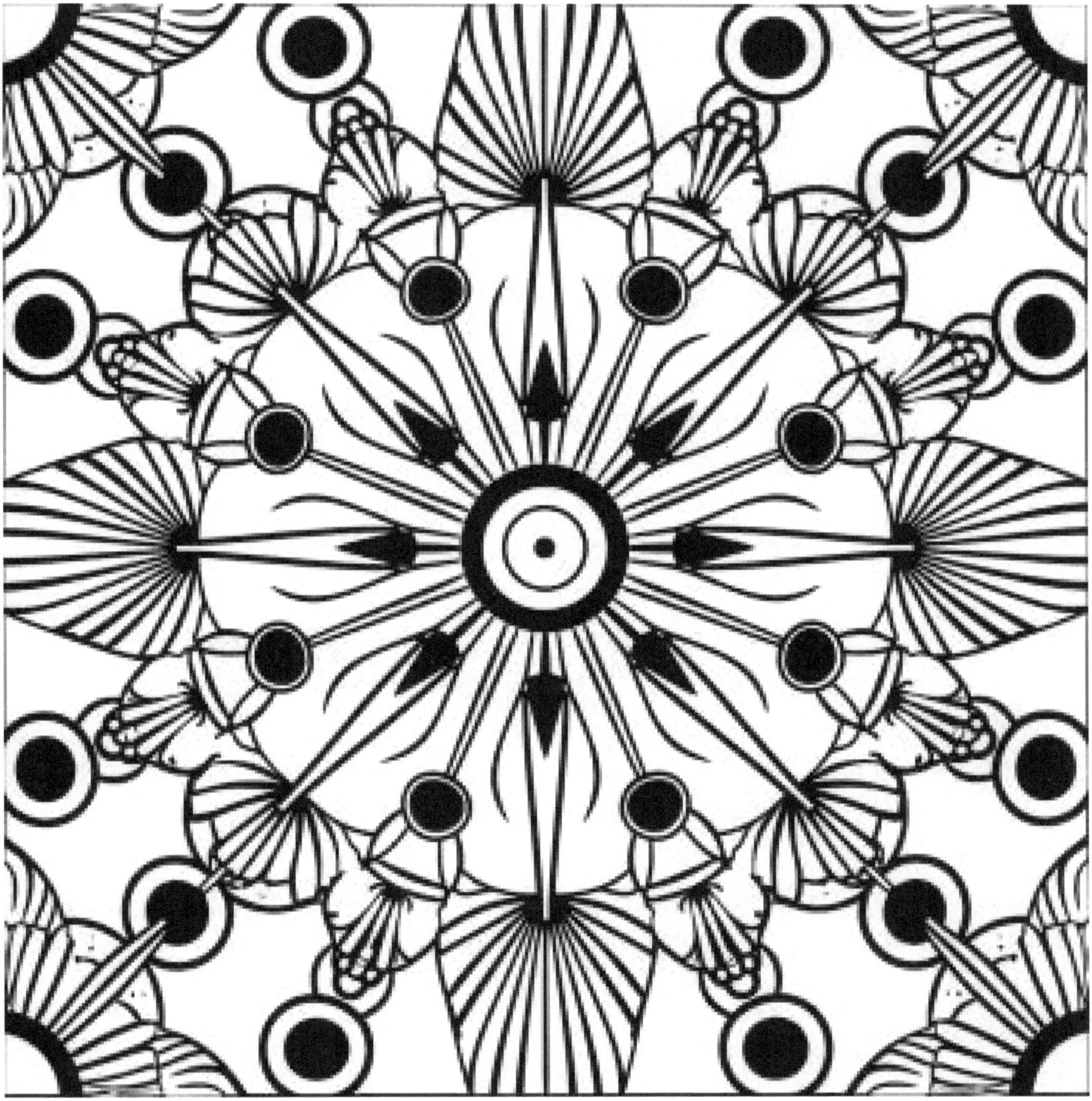

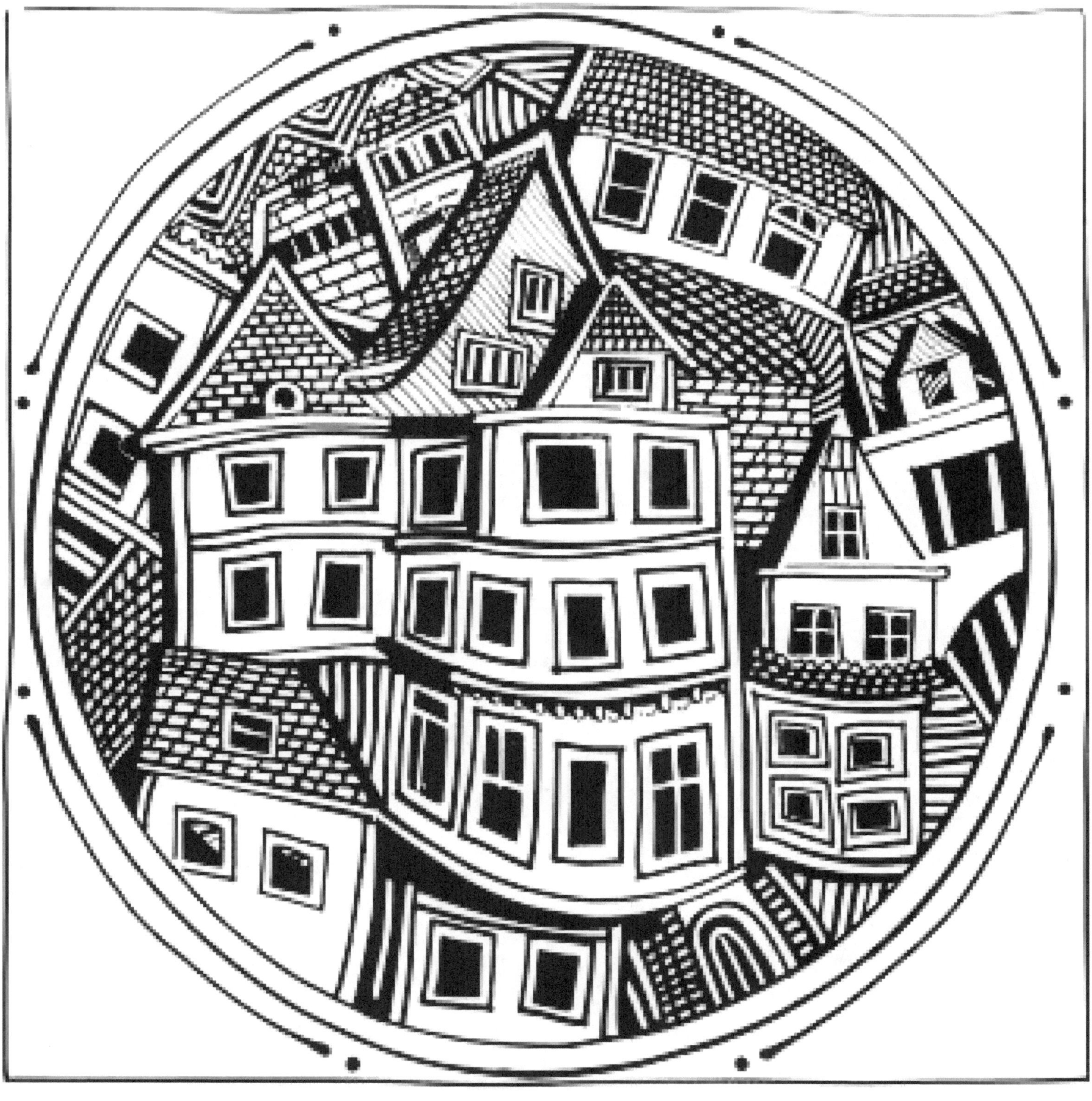

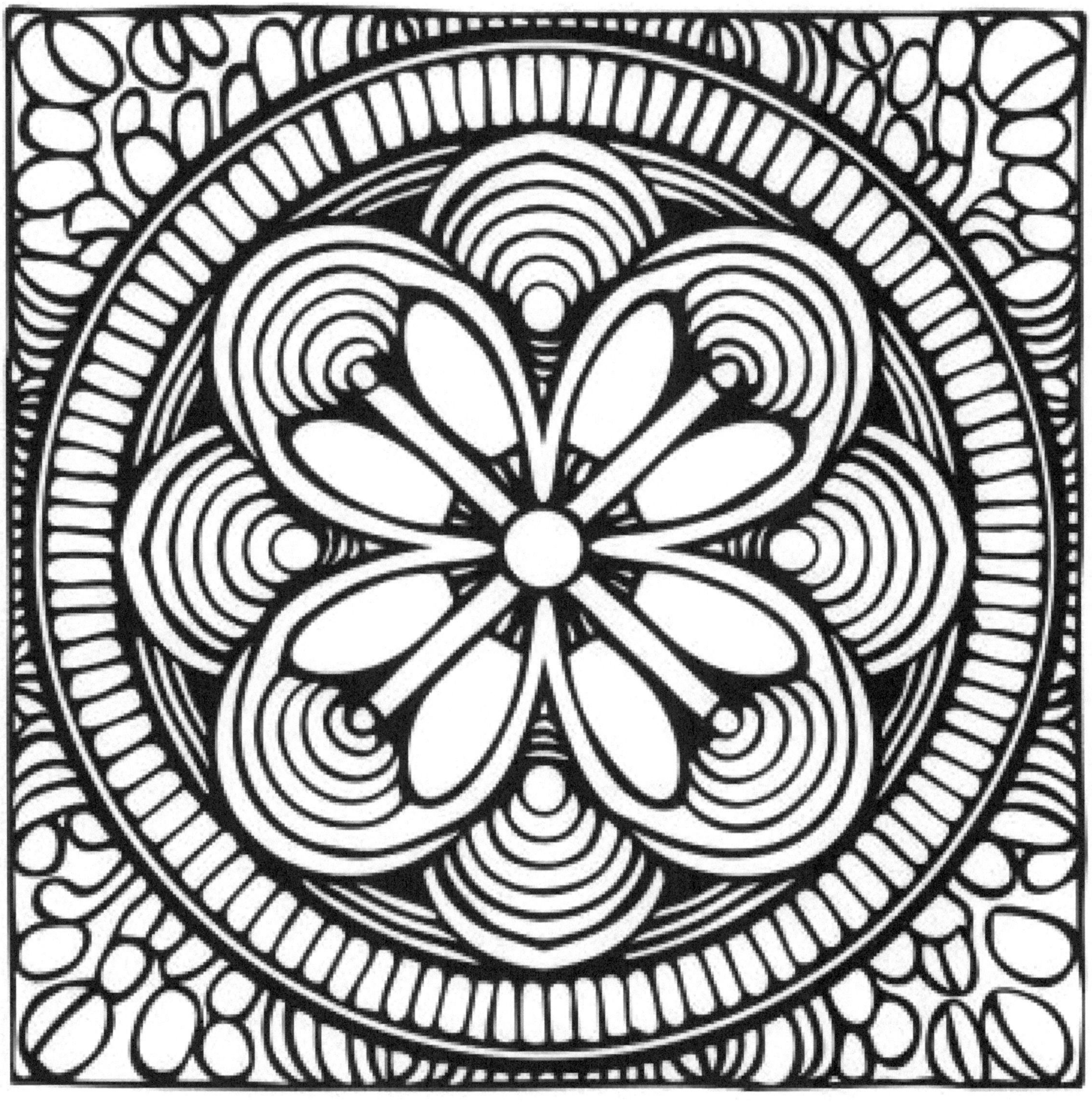

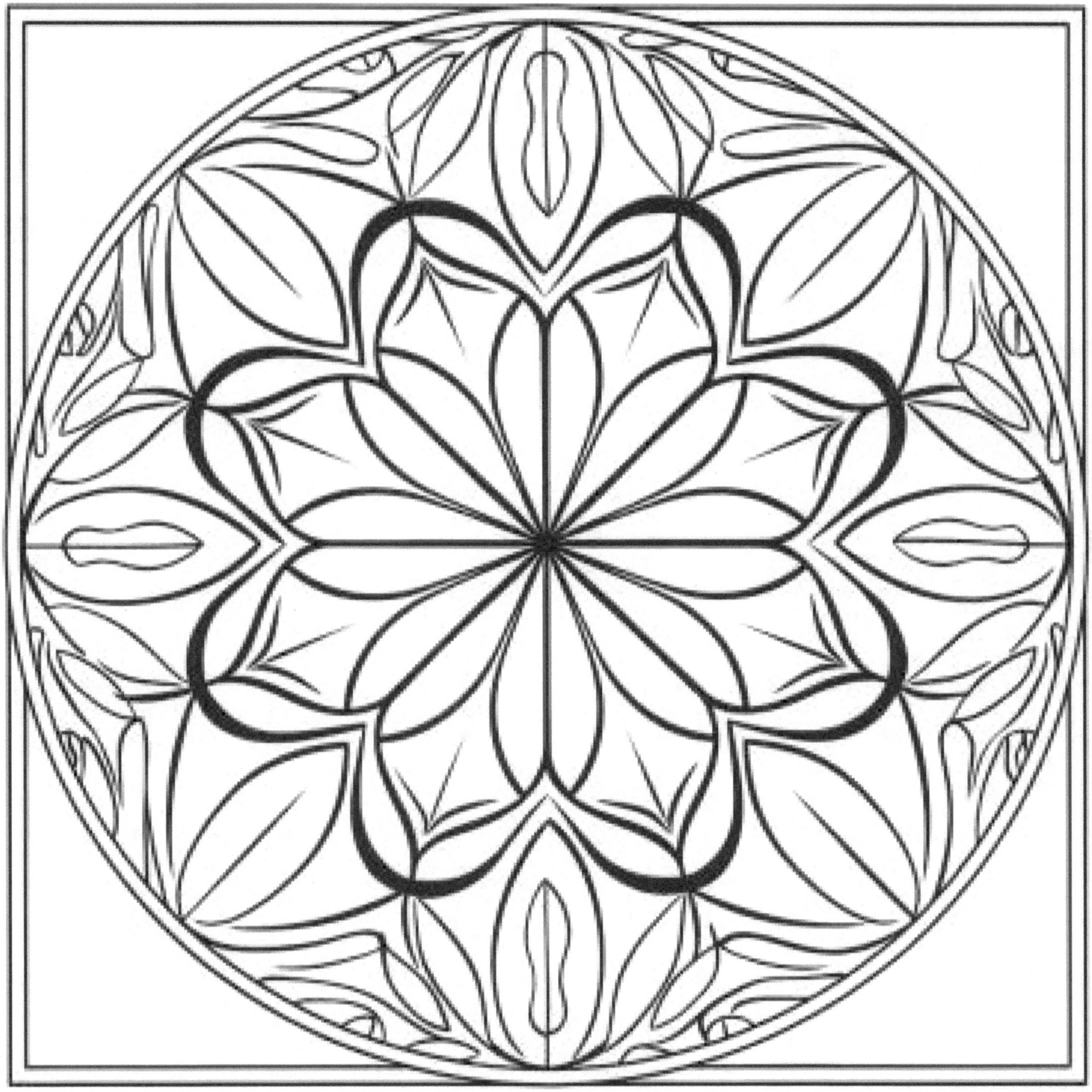

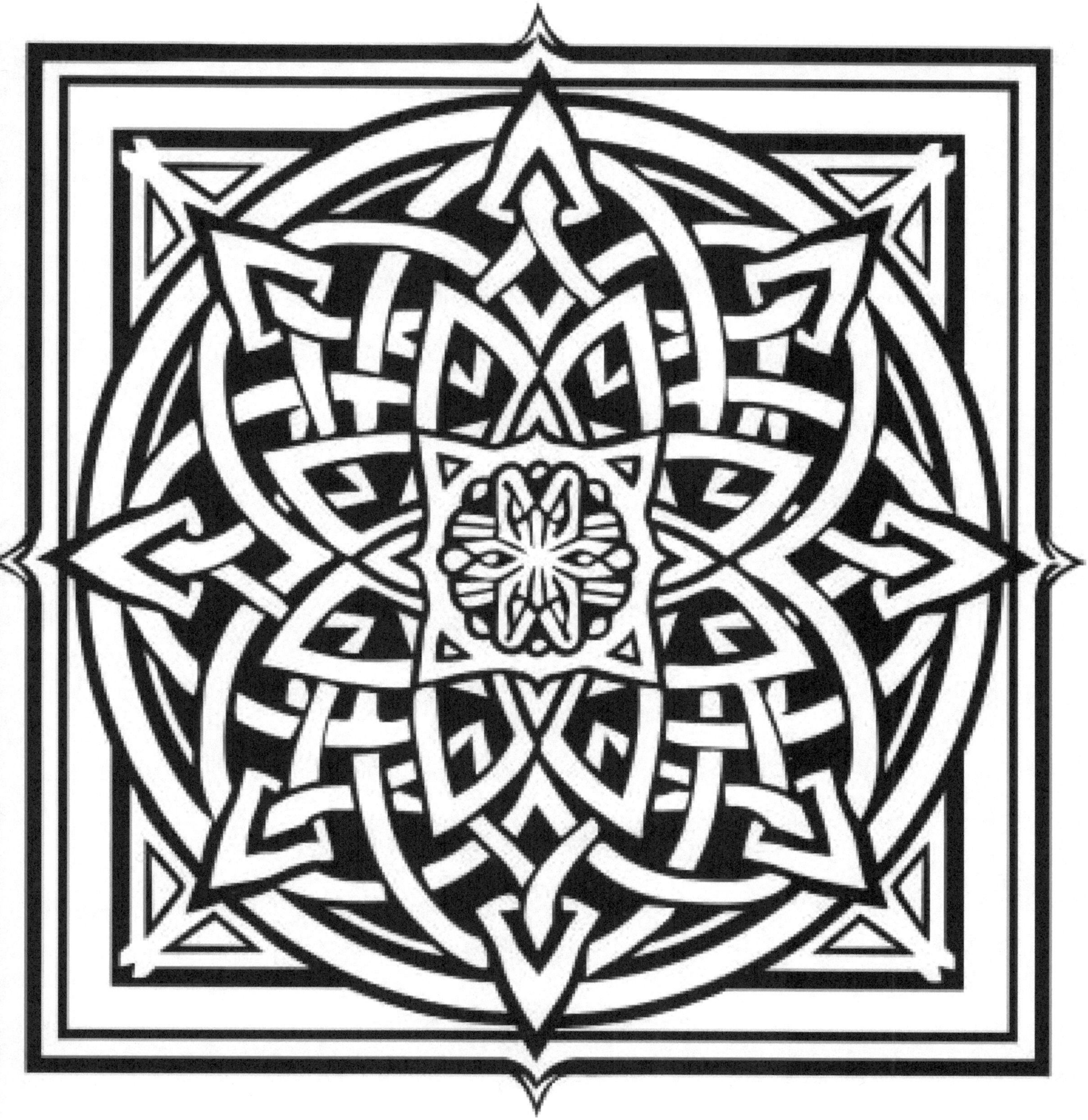

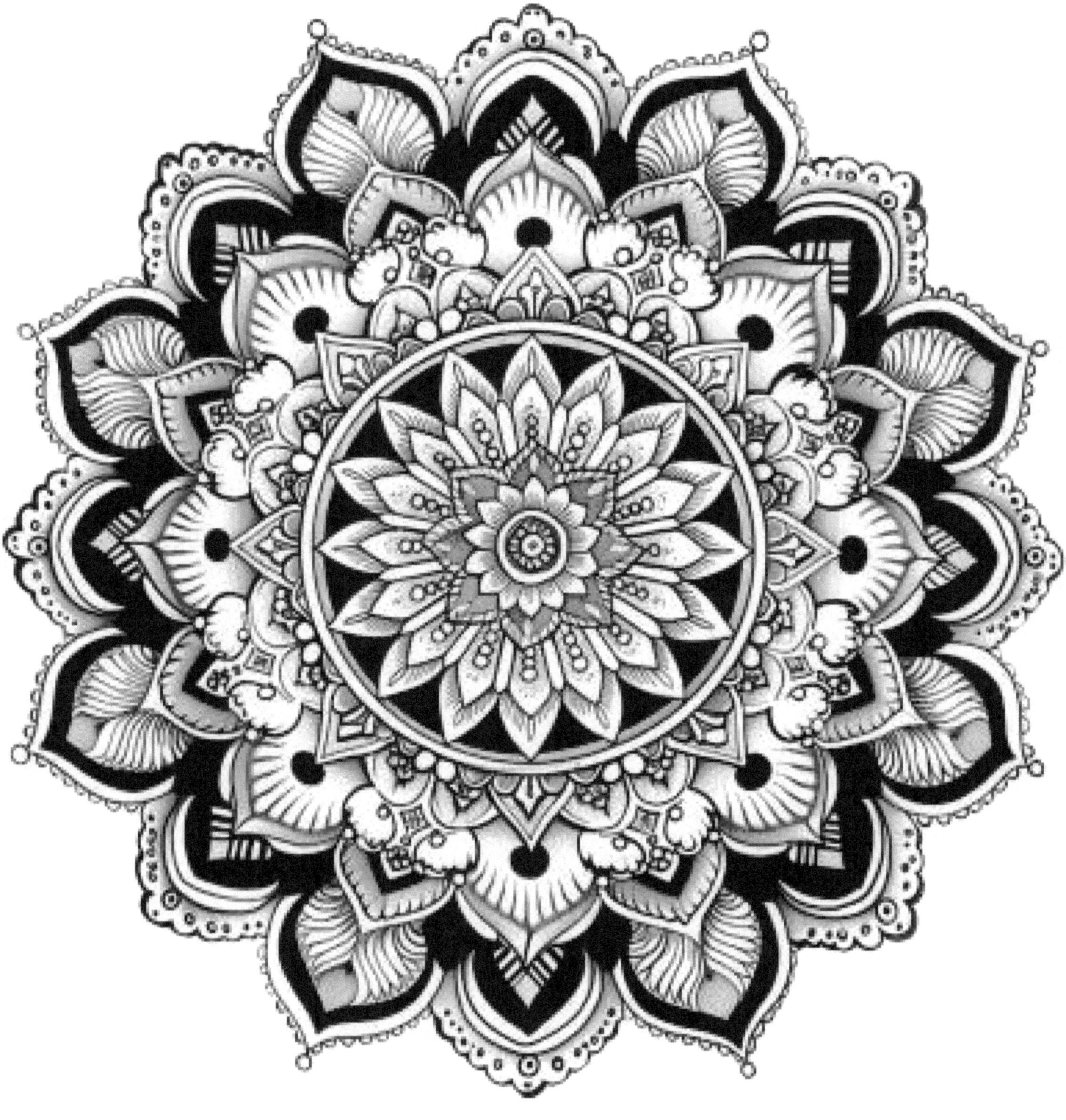

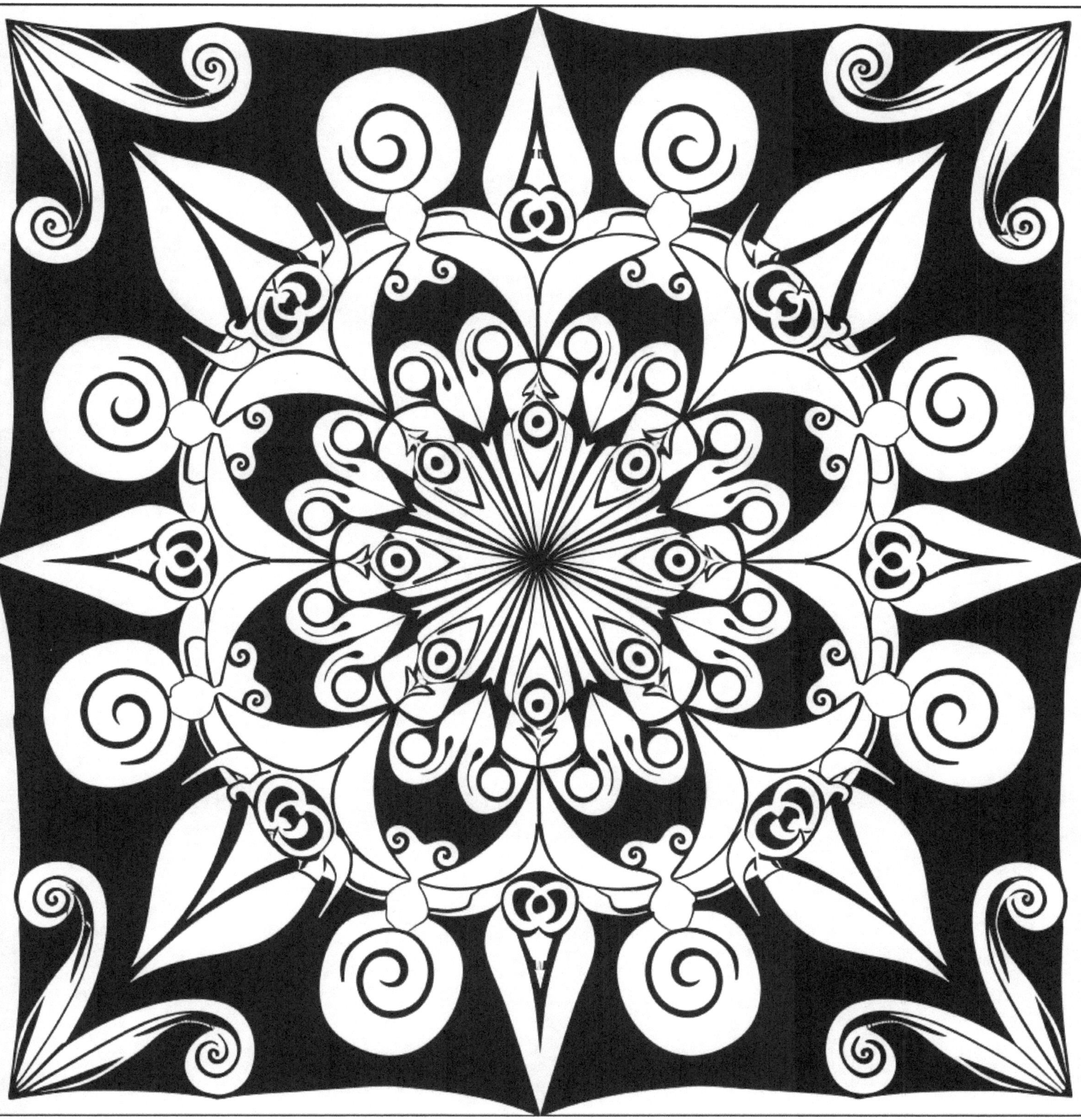

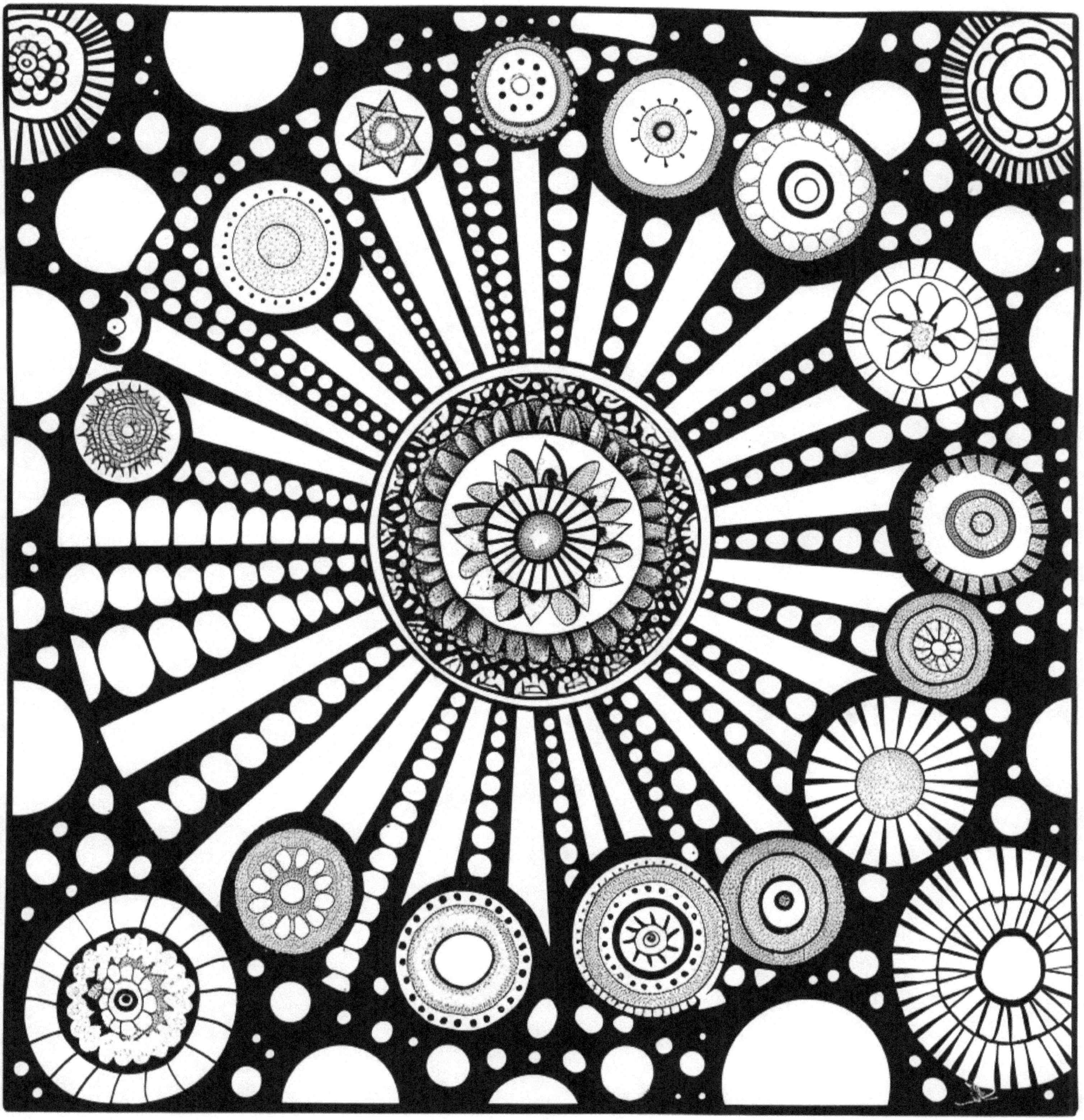

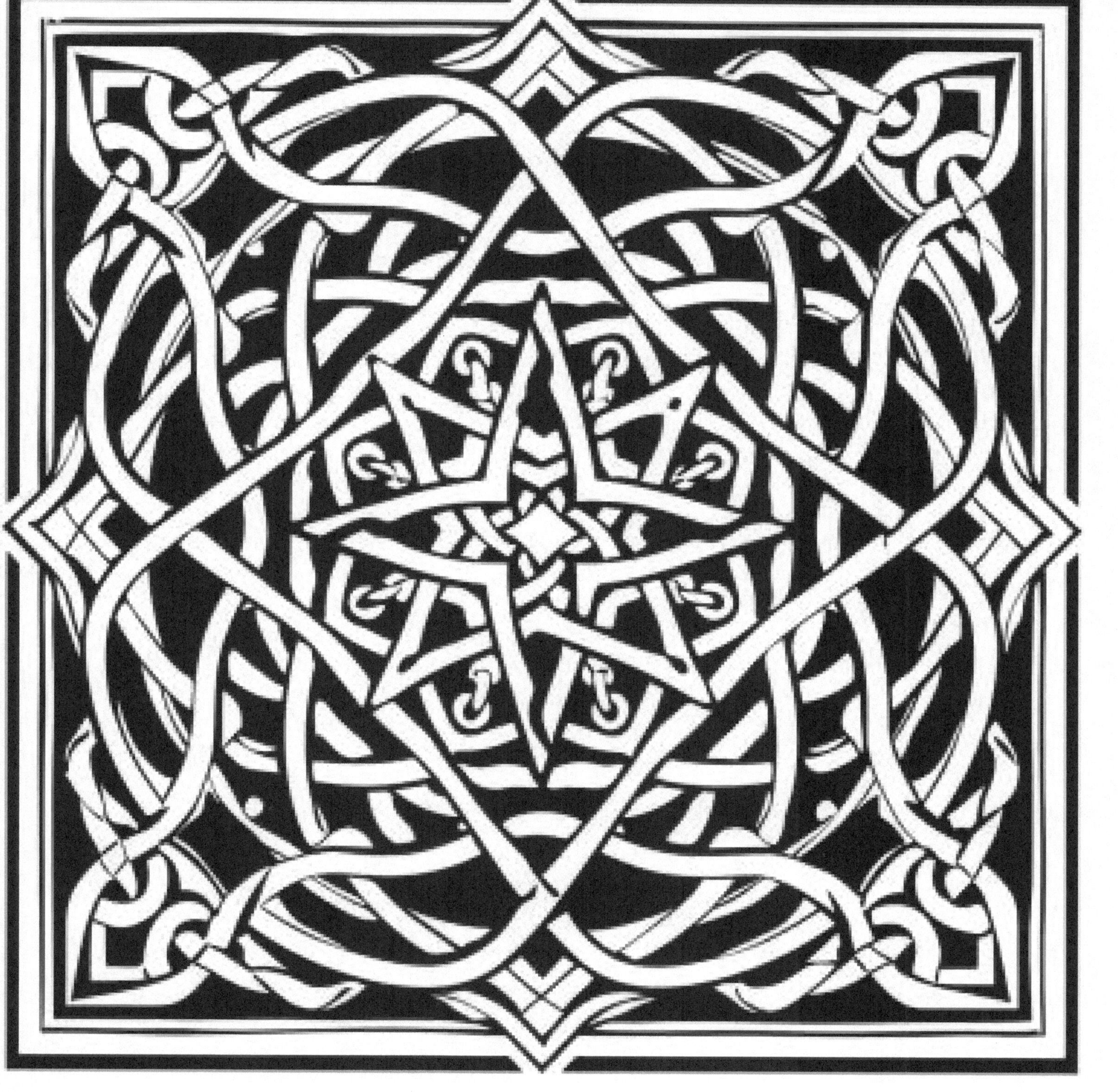

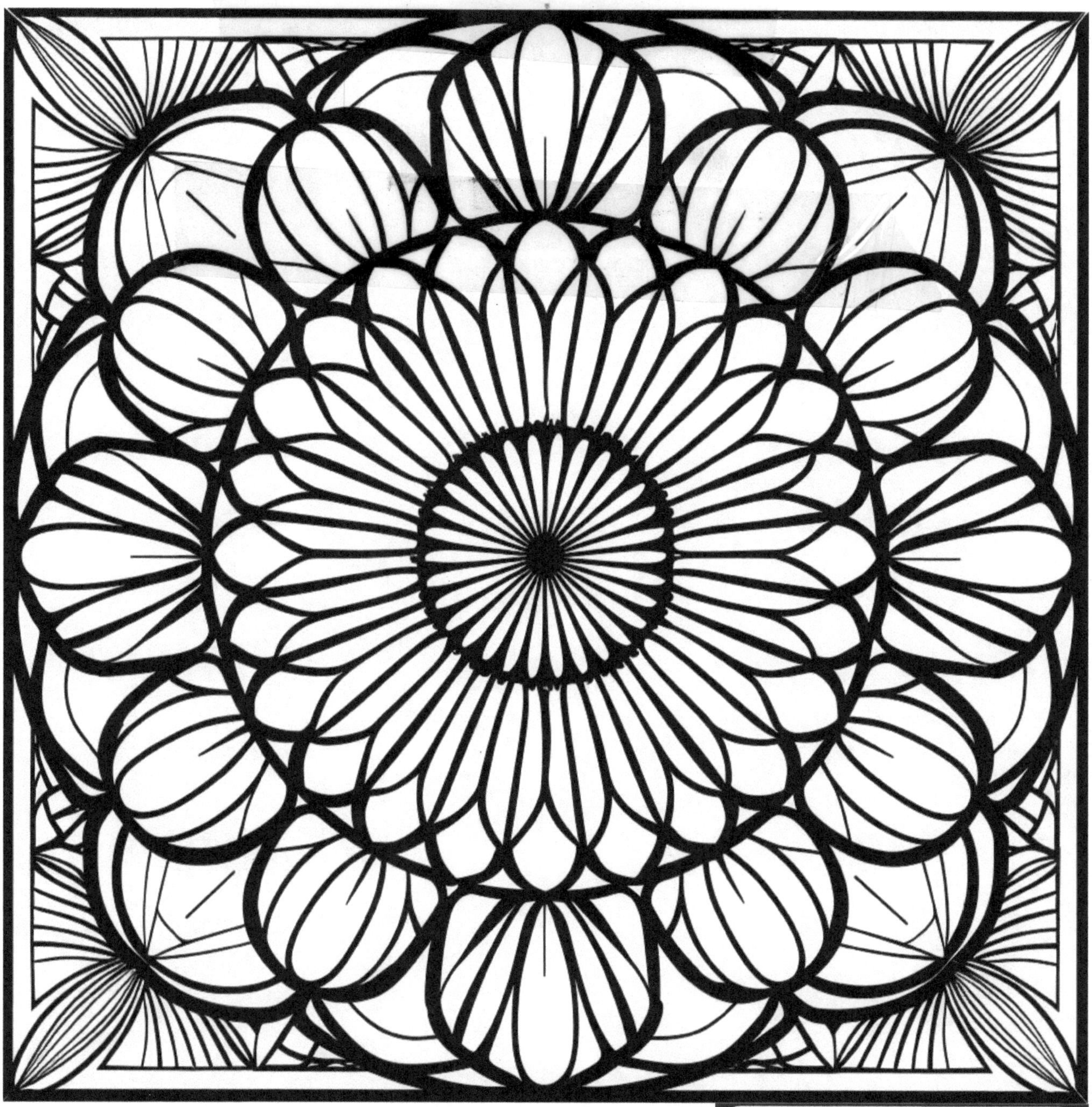

Thank You, share your experience with us and see you soon

@YANAGINTOVT

Made in United States
Troutdale, OR
06/01/2024

20262142R00058